ANIMAL FARM

George Orwell

AUTHORED by Tania Asnes
UPDATED AND REVISED by Adam Kissel

COVER DESIGN by Table XI Partners LLC
COVER PHOTO by Olivia Verma and © 2005 GradeSaver, LLC

BOOK DESIGN by Table XI Partners LLC

Published by GradeSaver LLC, www.gradesaver.com

First published in the United States of America by GradeSaver LLC. 2008

ISBN 978-1-60259-132-5

Printed in the United States of America

For other products and additional information please visit http://www.gradesaver.com

Table of Contents

Table of Contents

Biography of George Orwell (1903-1950)

George Orwell is the pen name of Eric Arthur Blair: essayist, novelist, literary critic, advocate and fighter for political change, and man of contradictions. Blair was born on June 25, 1903, in the Bengal region of Eastern India, which was a British territory. He was the son of Richard Walmesley Blair, a civil servant, and Ida Mabel Blair. Their only son was the middle child. He moved to England with his mother and sisters at the age of one. He displayed academic talent from a young age, so his mother took pains to ensure his attendance at a well-known boarding school called St. Cyprian's. His family was neither poor nor wealthy, and Blair attended St. Cyprian's on a scholarship.

Blair excelled academically there but faced many hardships in its puritanical, cutthroat environment. In the autobiographical essay "Such, Such Were the Joys," Blair/Orwell describes the social challenges he endured as a scholarship student among England's wealthy elite. (These challenges would inform his satires of social stratification in his literary works, including Animal Farm.) In the essay, he describes his child self with much sympathy and feeling for the child's perspective. Such experiments in empathy prepared him to create Animal Farm's brilliantly naive narrator.

Blair's academic prowess continued in secondary school at Eton, a renowned secondary school (more recently famous for Prince William's attendance there). Blair graduated from Eton in 1921. Despite his intelligence, he could not afford to attend college. In 1922, he joined the Indian Imperial Police in Burma. He had spent the first year of his life in a British colony, and this time, he got a thorough experience of British colonial life and despised what he saw. His experiences made him a champion of the poor and downtrodden, a role in which he would continue for the rest of his life. Moreover, he could not stand the fact that his job put him directly in the position of privileged oppressor. He resigned from the Indian Imperial Police five years later while on leave in England.

Blair/Orwell thus became devoted to the problems of class and government power long before he wrote Animal Farm. As Louis Menand writes, "He turned his life into an experiment in classlessness, and the intensity of his commitment to that experiment was the main reason that his friends and colleagues found him a perverse and sometimes exasperating man." To complete his rejection of elitism, Blair lived after the fashion of the poorest Englanders. This included refusing to wear warm clothing in winter or to display table manners. It is questionable whether his destitute lifestyle contributed to his frequent illnesses, but such choices indubitably influenced his written works.

Blair tried his luck in Paris briefly but found he could not make a living there as a writer. He returned to England in 1929, where he published essays and continued his fascination with and incorporation into the dregs of society. He began to slip into poverty in earnest, so he took a job as a teacher at Frays College. He also secured himself a literary agent. Blair/Orwell published *Down and Out in Paris* in 1932. Before the book's publication, Blair assumed the pen name by which he would become famous. Accounts of why the writer chose the pen name "George Orwell" vary. Some say the name is deeply symbolic while others state that it was merely one of a list of names from which he allowed his publishers to choose.

From 1934 on, Orwell thrust himself fully into the writer's arena. He quit his teaching job and moved to Hempstead, an epicenter for young writers at the time, where he worked in a used-book store. He published his first fictional work, *Burmese Days*, in 1934, and followed with *A Clergyman's Daughter* in 1935. Orwell's presence in Hempstead and his interest in the lower class did not go unnoticed. In 1936, the Left Book Club commissioned him to write an account of the destitute state of Northern England. Orwell threw himself into the project, conducting firsthand research in his quest for authenticity. In his travels, he met and married Eileen O'Shaughnessy. The controversial account was published in 1936 under the name *The Road to Wigan Pier*. He published *Aspidistra Flying* in the same year.

Around the time *The Road to Wigan Pier* was published, Orwell took his offensive against elitism and tyranny a step further, volunteering to fight in the Spanish Civil War on the side of the Republicans. He joined POUM, a Trotskyist socialist party that emphasized the need for a working-class uprising and opposed the Spanish Communist Party's belief in collaborating with the middle class (Orwell was a revolutionary socialist). Orwell's experiences in the war, including being shot almost fatally, cemented his hatred of totalitarianism in its many guises. This included Stalinism, against which he held a lifetime grudge. Ironically, Orwell's neck injury very nearly—and literally—robbed the outspoken writer of his voice. However, he did recover, and while doing so Orwell completed a novel, *Coming Up for Air*. Orwell described his social observations of Spain in *Homage to Catalonia*.

In 1940, Orwell and his wife moved to central London, where he worked as a reviewer. When World War II began, he rose to fight for the cause of freedom again, this time for England. He joined the Home Guard and worked for the BBC to compose and disseminate wartime propaganda. Orwell knew of what he spoke when he skewered propaganda in Animal Farm and 1984. Orwell based his satires not just on hearsay and research but also on personal experience; writing propaganda is said to have made him feel corrupt.

He was also a war correspondent. During wartime, Orwell and his wife adopted a son, but his wife died shortly afterwards. Also during this time, Orwell completed Animal Farm, which was published in England in 1945. It was at this point, just when Orwell's personal life was in shambles, that his legend took flight. The book met with immediate and far-reaching public success, especially since it was so topical.

Orwell continued to write for periodicals while completing his second renowned novel, 1984. He remarried, in 1949, to Sonia Brownell.

Orwell, who was prone to illness, had his career and his life cut short when he died of tuberculosis on January 21, 1950. His friend, David Astor, arranged for Orwell's burial in a small county churchyard. Orwell is buried under his birth name. He left a strong literary and political legacy, being one of those artists who influenced not only the literary universe, but also the real world in which he lived. As he wrote in "Politics and the English Language": "In our age there is no such thing as 'keeping out of politics.' All issues are political issues, and politics itself is a mass of lies, evasions, folly, hatred and schizophrenia." This statement also illustrates the pessimism for which Orwell was known. Like some other disillusioned people of his generation, Orwell believed that totalitarian governments would inevitably take over the West.

About Animal Farm

Animal Farm was published on the heels of World War II, in England in 1945 and in the United States in 1946. George Orwell wrote the book during the war as a cautionary fable in order to expose the seriousness of the dangers posed by Stalinism and totalitarian government. Orwell faced several obstacles in getting the novel published. First, he was putting forward an anti-Stalin book during a time when Western support for the Soviet Union was still high due to its support in Allied victories against Germany. Second, Orwell was not yet the literary star he would quickly become. For those reasons, Animal Farm appeared only at the war's end, during the same month that the United States dropped atomic bombs on Hiroshima and Nagasaki. The tragically violent events of the war set the stage well for Orwell's fictional manifesto against totalitarianism.

Animal Farm was Orwell's first highly successful novel (the second being 1984), and it helped launch him out of the minor fame of an essayist into the stratosphere of acclaimed fiction. Despite publishers' initial hesitance toward the book, the public in both Britain and the United States met it with enthusiasm. In the United States alone, it sold 600,000 copies in four years. Animal Farm was translated into many languages, proving its universal reach.

Animal Farm is an allegory or fable, a fairy tale for adults. Orwell uses animal characters in order to draw the reader away from the world of current events into a fantasy space where the reader can grasp ideas and principles more crisply. At the same time, Orwell personifies the animals in the tradition of allegory so that they symbolize real historical figures. In their own universe, people can become desensitized even to terrible things like deception, mistreatment, and violence. By demonstrating how these things occur in an allegorical world, Orwell makes them more clearly understood in the real world. For instance, in Animal Farm's public execution, Orwell lays bare the matter of execution by having the dogs rip out the supposed traitors' throats. In this scene, the reader is led to focus not as much on the means of execution as on the animalistic, atrocious reality of execution itself.

Animal Farm is also a powerful satire. Orwell uses irony to undermine the tenets of totalitarianism, specifically that of Stalinism.

Almost instantly after the novel's publication, it became the subject of revisionism. In one instance, the CIA made an animated film version of the book in which they eliminated the final scene and replaced it with a new revolution in which the animals overthrow the pigs (see the 1999 Hallmark film version for another change in ending). They distributed the film as anti-communist propaganda, which is ironic when one considers the novel's own censure of the propagandist rewriting of history. This revision and others over the years (whether in changing the story or interpreting it) contributed to the public's general misunderstanding of Orwell. Though he was staunchly anti-Stalinist, he was certainly not a capitalist. In fact, he was a revolutionary socialist. During his lifetime, Orwell did little to detract from his skewed public image. He was a man of contradictions--Louis Menand calls him "a middle-class intellectual who despised the middle class and was contemptuous of intellectuals, a Socialist whose abuse of Socialists ... was as vicious as any Tory's."

Animal Farm is universally appealing for both the obvious and the subtle messages of the fable. While the allegory's characters and events are deeply or specifically symbolic, Orwell's narrator softens some of the punches by including a gentle and un-opinionated narrator. The third-person narrator is outside the animals' world, so he does not relate any of the lies, hardships, or atrocities firsthand. Rather, he is a quiet observer.

Moreover, the narrator relates the tale from the perspective of the animals other than the dogs and pigs. In this way, the narrator's approach to the story resembles Orwell's approach to life. That is, just as Orwell developed empathy for the working class by experiencing working-class life firsthand, the narrator's tale is based on the experience of someone who is not quite an insider but no longer just an outsider. The narrator's animal perspective, as well as his reluctance to opine, fits well with the naivete of the animal characters.

One example of the narrator's indifferent approach to the tale is evident when the pigs use the money from Boxer's slaughter to buy a case of whisky. Rather than relating this event in stark terms, the narrator states impartially that on the day appointed for Boxer's memorial banquet, a carton arrives at the farmhouse followed by loud singing and "the word went round that from somewhere or other the pigs had acquired the money to buy themselves another case of whisky" (126). The scene also exemplifies how the narrator's naïve perspective produces an drily ironic effect.

Here are two other examples of ironic humor in the novel. In Chapter I, the narrator describes "Beasts of England" as "a stirring tune, something between 'Clementine' and 'La Cucaracha'" (32). Anyone familiar with those two songs knows that they are childish ditties. In Chapter IX, the narrator reports that the pigs find "a large bottle of pink medicine" in the farmhouse's medicine cabinet. They send it out to Boxer, who is deathly ill. We can assume that the medicine, being pink, is the antacid Pepto-Bismol, hardly useful to someone on his deathbed. By lightening his allegory with ironic humor, Orwell makes the story more palatable without taking away from his message.

Character List

Benjamin

The donkey. He is the oldest animal on the farm and stereotypically stubborn and crotchety. He is also intelligent, being the only animal (aside from the pigs) that can read fluently. He never laughs, preferring to make cynical comments, especially the cryptic line, "donkeys live a long time." Despite Benjamin's unfriendly nature, he has a special affinity for Boxer. The Rebellion does not change Benjamin's personality, although he eventually helps the animals read the lettering on the side of the van and the maxim that replaces the Seven Commandments. Benjamin represents the human (and also stereotypically Russian) tendency towards apathy; he holds fast to the idea that life is inherently hard and that efforts for change are futile. Benjamin bears a similarity to Orwell himself. Over the course of his career, Orwell became politically pessimistic and predicted the overtake of the West by totalitarian governments.

Bluebell, Jessie, and Pincher

The dogs. When Bluebell and Jessie give birth to puppies, Snowball confiscates them and secludes them in a loft, where he transforms them into fierce, elitist guard dogs.

Boxer

The male of the two horses on the farm. He is "an enormous beast, nearly eighteen hands high, and as strong as any two ordinary horses put together. A white stripe down his nose gave him a somewhat stupid appearance, and in fact he was not of first-rate intelligence, but he was universally respected for his steadiness of character and tremendous powers of work" (26). Boxer has a special affinity for Benjamin. With his determination to be a good public servant and his penchant for hard work, Boxer becomes Napoleon's greatest supporter. He works tirelessly for the cause of Animal Farm, operating under his personal maxims, "I will work harder" and "Napoleon is always right." The only time Boxer doubts propaganda is when Squealer tries to rewrite the story of Snowball's valor at the Battle of the Cowshed, a "treachery" for which he is nearly executed. But Boxer recants his doubts when he learns that the altered story of the battle is directly from Napoleon. After Boxer is injured while defending the farm in the Battle of the Windmill, Napoleon sends him to be slaughtered for profit. The pigs use the money from the slaughter to buy themselves a case of whisky. Boxer is not pugnacious despite his name, but he is as strong as his name implies. In this way, Boxer is a painfully ironic character. He is strong enough to kill another animal, even a human, with a single blow from his hoof, and the dogs cannot manage to overpower him in Chapter VII. Still, Boxer lacks the intelligence and the nerve to sense that he is being used. Boxer represents the peasant or working class, a faction of humanity with a great combined strength--enough to overthrow a manipulative government--but which is uneducated enough to take propaganda to heart and believe unconditionally in the government's cause.

the Cat

The only cat on Manor Farm. She is lazy and indifferent, but she does participate in the Battle of the Cowshed.

Clover

The female of the two horses on the farm. She is "a stout motherly mare approaching middle life, who had never quite got her figure back after her fourth foal." Clover is Boxer's faithful companion as well as a motherly figure to the other animals. Like Boxer, Clover is not intelligent enough to read, so she enlists Muriel to read the altered Seven Commandments to her. She sees the incongruities in the government's policies and actions, but she is not smart or defiant enough to fight for the restoration of justice. Clover represents those people who remember a time before the Revolution and therefore half-realize that the government is lying about its success and adherence to its principles, but are helpless to change anything.

the Dogs

Nine puppies, which Napoleon confiscates and secludes in a loft. Napoleon rears them into fierce, elitist dogs that act as his security guards. The dogs are the only animals other than the pigs that are given special privileges. They also act as executioners, tearing out the throats of animals that confess to treachery. The dogs represent the NKVD and more specifically the KGB, agencies Joseph Stalin fostered and used to terrorize and commit atrocities upon the Soviet Union's populace.

Frederick

The owner of Pinchfield, the small farm adjacent to Manor Farm. He is a hard-nosed individual who is known for his frequent legal troubles and demanding business style. He cheats the animals out of their timber by paying for it with fake banknotes. Frederick represents Adolf Hitler. Rumors of the exotic and cruel animal tortures Frederick enacts on his farm are meant to echo the horror stories emerging from Nazi Germany. Frederick's agreement to buy the timber represents the Nazi-Soviet non-aggression treaty, and his subsequent betrayal of the pact and invasion of Animal Farm represents the Nazi invasion of the Soviet Union.

Jones

The owner of Manor Farm and a drunkard. His animals overthrow him in the Rebellion. When he tries to recapture his property, they defeat him, steal his gun, and drive him off again. Mr. Jones dies in a home for alcoholics in another part of the country. He represents the kind of corrupt and fatally flawed government that results in discontent and revolution among the populace. More specifically, Jones represents the latter days of imperial Russia and its last leader, the wealthy but ineffective Czar Nicholas II.

Minimus

A pig with "a remarkable gift for composing songs and poems." Under Napoleon's rule, Minimus sits with him and Squealer on the barn platform during meetings. Minimus composes propaganda songs and poems under Napoleon's rule. Though we never hear Minimus complain about his duties as propaganda writer, he represents the Soviet Union's artists, who were forced to use their talents to glorify communism rather than express their personal feelings or beliefs.

Mollie

The white mare that draws Mr. Jones's trap. Her personality is superficial and adolescent. For example, when she arrives at the big meeting in Chapter 1, Orwell writes, "Mollie ... Came mincing daintily in, chewing a lump of sugar. She took a place near the front and began flirting her white mane, hoping to draw attention to the red ribbons it was plaited with" (27). Mollie is the only animal not to fight in the Battle of the Cowshed, instead hiding in her stall. She eventually flees the farm and is last seen, bedecked in ribbons, eating sugar and letting her new owner stroke her nose. Mollie represents the class of nobles who, unwilling to conform to the new regime, fled Russia after the Revolution.

Moses

A tame raven that is Mr. Jones's "especial pet." He is a spy, a gossip, and a "clever talker" (37). He is also the only animal not present for Old Major's meeting. Moses gets in the way of the pigs' efforts to spread Animalism by inventing a story about an animal heaven called Sugarcandy Mountain. Moses disappears for several years during Napoleon's rule. When he returns, he still insists on the existence of Sugarcandy Mountain. Moses represents religion, which gives people hope of a better life in heaven. His name connects him to the Judeo-Christian religions specifically, but he can be said to represent the spiritual alternative in general. The pigs dislike Moses's stories of Sugarcandy Mountain, just as the Soviet government opposed religion, not wanting its people to subscribe to a system of belief outside of communism. Though the Soviet government suppressed religion aggressively, the pigs on Animal Farm let Moses come and go as he pleases and even give him a ration of beer when he returns from his long absence.

Muriel

The white goat. Muriel can read fairly well and helps Clover decipher the alterations to the Seven Commandments. Muriel is not opinionated, but she represents a subtle, revelatory influence because of her willingness to help bring things to light (as opposed to Benjamin).

Napoleon

One of the leaders among the pigs, Napoleon is a "large, rather fierce-looking Berkshire boar" that is up for sale. He is the only Berkshire boar on the farm. He is "not much of a talker" and has "a reputation for getting his own way" (35). Napoleon expels Snowball from the farm and takes over. He modifies his opinions and policies and rewrites history continually to benefit the pigs. Napoleon awards special privileges to the pigs and especially to himself. For example, he dines on Mr. Jones's fine china, wears Mr. Jones's dress clothes, and smokes a pipe. As time goes on, Napoleon becomes a figure in the shadows, increasingly secluding himself and making few public appearances. Eventually, Napoleon holds a conciliatory meeting with the neighboring human farmers and effectively takes over Mr. Jones's position as dictator. Napoleon represents the type of dictator or tyrant who shirks the common good, instead seeking more and more power in order to create his own regime. Orwell reflects Napoleon's greed for power with a name that invokes Napoleon Bonaparte, the very successful French leader who became "Emperor" and brashly invaded Russia before being defeated by Russia. But Napoleon the pig more directly represents Stalin in his constantly changing policies and actions, his secret activities, his intentional deception and manipulation of the populace, and his use of fear tactics and atrocities.

Old Major

A prize Middle White boar that the Joneses exhibited under the name "Willingdon Beauty." He is, "stout … But still a majestic-looking pig, with a wise and benevolent appearance" (26). In addition to his laurels in the exhibition world, Major is highly respected among his fellow farm animals. His age is twelve years, which makes him a senior among them, and he also claims to have had over four hundred children. He is the one who calls the meeting in the first chapter to discuss his strange dream. Major claims to "understand the nature of life on this earth as well as any animal now living" (28). Months after his death, the pigs disinter his skull and place it at the base of the flagpole beside the gun. Major symbolizes two historical figures. First, he represents Karl Marx, the father of Marxism. Marx's political hypotheses about working-class consciousness and division of labor worked infinitely better in theory than in practice, especially when corrupt leaders twisted them for their personal gain. Second, Major represents Vladimir Lenin, the foremost of the three authors of the Russian Revolution and the formation of the Soviet Union. Lenin died during the Soviet Union's early years, leaving Trotsky (Snowball) and Stalin (Napoleon) to vie for his leadership position.

Pilkington

The owner of Foxwood, the large, unkempt farm adjacent to Manor Farm. He is an easy-going man who prefers pursuing his hobbies to maintaining his land. At the book's end, Mr. Pilkington offers a toast to the future cooperation between human farms and Animal Farm. He also says he plans to emulate Animal Farm's low rations and long work hours. Pilkington can be seen to represent the Allies. Allied countries explored the possibility of trade with the Soviet Union in the years leading up to World War II but kept a watchful distance. Ominously, as Friedrich Hayek points out in The Road to Serfdom (1944), communist principles had strong proponents among many Allied nations as well. Pilkington's unwillingness to save Animal Farm from Frederick and his men parodies the Allies' initial hesitance to enter the War. Napoleon's and Pilkington's poker game at the end of the book suggests the beginnings of a power struggle that would later become the Cold War.

Pinkeye

A pig that Napoleon enlists as his taster, lest someone try to poison him.

the Sheep

The sheep are loyal to the tenets of Animal Farm, often breaking into a chorus of "Four legs good, two legs bad" and later, "Four legs good, two legs better!" The Sheep--true to the typical symbolic meaning of "sheep"--represent those people who have little understanding of their situation and thus are willing to follow their government blindly.

Snowball

One of the leaders among the pigs, Snowball is a young pig that is up for sale. He is more intelligent than Napoleon but lacks Napoleon's depth of character. He is also a brilliant orator. Snowball, who represents Leon Trotsky, is a progressive politician and aims to improve Animal Farm with a windmill and other technological advances, but Napoleon expels him before he can do so. In his absence, Snowball comes to represent an abstract idea of evil. The animals blame misfortunes on him, including the windmill's destruction, and entertain the idea that he is lurking on one of the neighboring farms, plotting revenge. Napoleon uses the animals' fear of Snowball to create new propaganda and changes history to make it seem as though Snowball was always a spy and a traitor. Snowball's name is symbolic in this way. Napoleon encourages the animals' fear of him to grow or snowball so that it becomes so great it is almost palpable. Snowball's name may also refer to Trotsky's call (following Marx) to encourage a revolution outside the Soviet Union that would "snowball" into an international proletariat revolution. Snowball can more generally be said to represent systems of belief outside of communism, which the government demonizes in order to lionize its own system.

Squealer

The best known of the porker pigs, Squealer has "very round cheeks, twinkling eyes, nimble movements, and a shrill voice." He is also "a brilliant talker" who is talented in the art of argument. The other pigs say Squealer "could turn black into white" (35). Under Napoleon's rule, Squealer acts as the liaison to the other animals. He lies to them, rewriting history and reading them encouraging, but false, statistics. Squealer is especially good at playing on the animals' ignorance and gullibility. He represents the propaganda machine of a totalitarian government.

Whymper

A solicitor in Willingdon who acts as Animal Farm's intermediary to the human world. He is "a sly-looking little man with side whiskers." He visits the farm every Monday to get his orders and is paid in commissions. Mr. Whymper's business-minded attitude towards Animal Farm, which allows him to ignore the injustices and atrocities committed there, make him a parody of nations that conducted business with the Soviet Union while turning a blind eye to its internal affairs.

Major Themes

The Soviet Union under Stalinism

Animal Farm is a satire of totalitarian governments in their many guises. But Orwell composed the book for a more specific purpose: to serve as a cautionary tale about Stalinism. It was for this reason that he faced such difficulty in getting the book published; by the time *Animal Farm* was ready to meet its readers, the Allies were cooperating with the Soviet Union. The allegorical characters of the novel represent specific historical figures and different factions of Imperial Russian and Soviet society. These include Karl Marx (Major), Vladimir Lenin (Major), Leon Trotsky (Snowball), Joseph Stalin (Napoleon), Adolf Hitler (Frederick), the Allies (Pilkington), the peasants (Boxer), the elite (Mollie), and the church (Moses).

The resemblance of some of the novel's events to events in Soviet history is indubitable. For example, Snowball's and Napoleon's power struggle is a direct allegory of Trotsky's and Stalin's. Frederick's trade agreement with Napoleon, and his subsequent breaking of the agreement, represents the Nazi-Soviet non-aggression pact that preceded World War II. The following Battle of the Windmill represents World War II itself.

Despite his fairy-tale clarity in satirizing some historical events, Orwell is less specific about others. For example, the executions in Chapter VII conflate the Red Terror with the Great Purge. The executions themselves bear resemblance to both events, although their details connect them more to the Moscow Trials than to the Red Terror. Squealer's subsequent announcement that the executions have ended the Rebellion connects them to the period of the Red Terror, however. Orwell leaves some ambiguity in the identities of the Rebellion and the Battle of the Cowshed. These ambiguities help the reader focus on the overall satire of Stalinism and the broader warning about the evils of totalitarian government.

The Inevitability of Totalitarianism

Orwell held the pessimistic belief that totalitarianism was inevitable, even in the West. According to Russell Baker, who wrote the preface to *Animal Farm*'s 1996 Signet Classics version, Orwell's pessimism stemmed from his having grown up in an age of dictatorship. Witnessing Hitler's and Stalin's movements from afar, as well as fighting totalitarianism in the Spanish Civil War, Orwell came to believe in the rise of a new species of autocrat, worse even than the tyrants of old. This cynicism is reflected in both of his highly successful novels, *Animal Farm* and *1984*. Orwell emphasizes the insidiousness of totalitarianism early in the novel, when the pigs take the fresh milk and apples. The pigs justify their actions on the basis of their superiority; they are smart and need more nutrition than the other animals to fuel their brainpower. There is no scientific basis for the pigs' claim—in fact, if anyone needs more food to fuel their labor, it is the manual laborers—but they can count on the animals' being too ignorant to realize that. In this way, Orwell makes the point that totalitarianism need not be blatant in order to be operating. It can hide under the guise of the "greater good" as it did in the Soviet Union before the totalitarianism became obvious.

Orwell uses a cyclical structure in *Animal Farm*, which helps advance the idea of totalitarianism's predictability. The novel begins with Jones as autocratic tyrant and ends with Napoleon not only in Jones's position, but in his clothes as well. Over the course of the novel, Napoleon essentially becomes Jones just as Stalin becomes an autocrat after pretending to espouse equality and freedom. Orwell cements this idea in the book's final scene, where he writes, "Twelve voices were shouting in anger, and they were all alike. No question, now, what had happened to the faces of the pigs. The creatures outside looked from pig to man, and from man to pig, and from pig to man again; but already it was impossible to say which was which" (139). The circularity of Orwell's story prevents the reader from imagining a better future for Animal Farm. After all, even if another Rebellion were to take place, its leaders would eventually come to emulate Napoleon.

According to Baker, technology turned out to be the force freeing people from Orwell's age of dictators. But "technology" can be just another banner under which to rally the people. While Orwell does portray technology as a source of progress in *Animal Farm*, he points out that it is useless unless it is in the people's hands. Most notably, even when the windmill is finished it is used for milling corn instead of its original purpose of supplying the animals with electricity in their stalls.

Intelligence and Education as Tools of Oppression

From the very beginning of the novel, we become aware of education's role in stratifying Animal Farm's population. Following Major's death, the pigs are the ones that take on the task of organizing and mobilizing the other animals because they are "generally recognized as being the cleverest of the animals" (35). At first, the pigs are loyal to their fellow animals and to the revolutionary cause. They translate Major's vision of the future faithfully into the Seven Commandments of Animalism. However, it is not long before the pigs' intelligence and education turn from tools of enlightenment to implements of oppression. The moment the pigs are faced with something material that they want—the fresh milk—they abandon their morals and use their superior intellect and knowledge to deceive the other animals.

The pigs also limit the other animals' opportunities to gain intelligence and education early on. They teach themselves to read and write from a children's book but destroy it before the other animals can have the same chance. Indeed, most of the animals never learn more than a few letters of the alphabet. Once the pigs cement their status as the educated elite, they use their mental advantage to manipulate the other animals. For example, knowing that the other animals cannot read the Seven Commandments, they revise them whenever they like. The pigs also use their literacy to learn trades from manuals, giving them an opportunity for economic specialization and advancement. Content in the role of the intelligentsia, the pigs forgo manual labor in favor of bookkeeping and organizing. This shows that the pigs have not only the advantage of opportunity, but also the opportunity to reject whatever opportunities they like. The pigs' intelligence and education allow them to bring the other animals into submission through the use of propaganda and revisionism. At the book's end, we witness Napoleon's preparations to educate a new generation of pigs and indoctrinate them into the code of oppression.

Propaganda and Duplicity

Working as a propagandist during World War II, Orwell experienced firsthand both the immense power and the dishonesty of propaganda. Many types of governments make use of propaganda, not only totalitarian ones. Consider, for instance, the arguments that led many United States citizens to go along with the idea of invading Iraq after the September 11, 2001, terror attacks. Propaganda serves the positive task of uniting the people, sometimes at the cost of misleading them. Orwell takes a firm stance on the harmfulness of propaganda in *Animal Farm* while acknowledging its value for rallying a mistreated and disillusioned populace.

In Chapter IX, Orwell demonstrates the positive value of propaganda. By this point, the animals are so downtrodden that they are desperate for something in which to believe. (Note the irony, though: it is Napoleon who has robbed them of their belief in the original version of Animalism.) The falsely optimistic statistics, the songs, and especially the Spontaneous Demonstrations give the animals something to live for. This chapter is an exception in terms of portraying propaganda in a positive light. For the majority of *Animal Farm*, Orwell skewers propaganda and exposes its nature as deception.

Squealer represents a totalitarian government's propaganda machine. Eloquent to a fault, he can make the animals believe almost anything. This fact is especially clear in Squealer's interactions with Clover and Muriel. Each time Clover suspects that the Seven Commandments have been changed, Squealer manages to convince her that she is wrong. After the executions, Napoleon abolishes the singing of "Beasts of England" in favor of a new anthem, the lyrics of which contain a promise never to harm Animal Farm. In this propagandist maneuver, Napoleon replaces the revolutionary spirit of "Beasts of England" with the exact opposite, a promise not to rebel. In addition to being a source of manipulation, propaganda is an agent of fear and terror. Orwell demonstrates this quite clearly with Napoleon's vilification of Snowball and his assurances that Snowball could attack the animals at any minute. He uses similar fear tactics regarding Frederick and Pilkington. The most egregious example of propaganda in the novel is the maxim that replaces the Seven Commandments: "All animals are equal / But some animals are more equal than others." The idea of "more equal" is mathematically improbable and a nonsensical manipulation of language, but by this time, the animals are too brainwashed to notice.

Violence and Terror as Means of Control

In *Animal Farm,* Orwell criticizes the ways that dictators use violence and terror to frighten their populaces into submission. Violence is one of the yokes from which the animals wish to free themselves when they prepare for the Rebellion. Not only does Jones overwork the animals and steal the products of their labor, but he can whip or slaughter them at his discretion. Once the pigs gain control of the animals, they, like Jones, discover how useful violence and terror can be. They use this knowledge to their full advantage. The foremost example of violence and terror in the novel is the pattern of public executions. The executions can be said to represent both the Red Terror and the Great Purge, but they stand more broadly for the abuse of power. For example, they are also similar to the Taliban's public executions in Kabul's soccer stadium in modern Afghanistan.

Capital punishment for criminals is a hotly debated issue. Killing *suspected* criminals, as Napoleon does, is quite another issue. The executions perhaps best symbolize the Moscow Trials, which were show trials that Stalin arranged to instill fear in the Soviet people. To witnesses at the time, the accused traitors' confessions seemed to be given freely. In fact, they were coerced. Napoleon likely coerces confessions from many of the animals that he executes. Orwell's use of the allegory genre serves him well in the execution scene. Execution with weapons is a violent and horrifying act, but many people have become desensitized to it. Orwell's allegorical executioners, the dogs that kill cruelly, portray the bloody and inescapably animalistic side of execution.

Terror comes also in threats and propaganda. Each time the animals dare to question an aspect of Napoleon's regime, Squealer threatens them with Jones's return. This is doubly threatening to the animals because it would mean another battle that, if lost, would result in a return to their former lifestyle of submission. Jones's return is such a serious threat that it quashes the animals' curiosity without fail. The other major example of fear tactics in the novel is the threat of Snowball and his collaborators. Napoleon is able to vilify Snowball in the latter's absence and to make the animals believe that his return, like Jones's, is imminent. Snowball is a worse threat than Jones, because Jones is at least safely out of Animal Farm. Snowball is "proved" to be not only lurking along Animal Farm's borders but infiltrating the farm. Napoleon's public investigation of Snowball's whereabouts cements the animals' fear of Snowball's influence. In modern language, Snowball is pegged as the terrorist responsible for the infringements on the rights and liberties instigated by the pigs.

Exploitation and the Need for Human Rights

Exploitation is the issue around which the animals unite. Initially, the animals do not realize Jones is exploiting them. For this reason, Old Major's speech is a revelation of momentous proportions. Major explains to the animals that they are enslaved and exploited and that Man is to blame. He teaches them not only what exploitation means, but also the fact that it is not inevitable. Orwell suggests that exploitation is, in fact, bound to happen when one class of society has an advantage over another. The opposite of exploitation, according to Major, is the state of being "rich and free." Major's ideas about animal rights symbolize the importance—and scarcity—of human rights in an oppressive regime. Gaining freedom does not necessarily lead people also to become rich, but it is better to be poor and free than poor and exploited.

All the animals on Animal Farm are exploited under Napoleon's control, save the pigs. Even the dogs, which work closely with the pigs, are exploited. The dogs face perhaps even a worse form of exploitation than the other animals, because they are made into agents of intimidation and death. Whereas Napoleon exploits the other animals' physical strength and their ignorance, he exploits the dogs' viciousness and turns them into villains against their parents' wishes.

Boxer's life is a particularly sad example of exploitation because he exploits himself, believing wholeheartedly in Napoleon's goodness. In the end, Napoleon turns the tables and exploits Boxer, having him slaughtered for profit. By the end of the novel, we see clearly how the animals participate in their own exploitation. They are beginning to build a schoolhouse for the thirty-one young pigs Napoleon has fathered (perhaps an oblique reference to the "Thirty Tyrants" of ancient Greece). That schoolhouse will never benefit the animals that build it; rather, it will be used to educate the pigs and indoctrinate them into the cycle of exploiting others. Throughout the novel, Orwell shows us how the lack of human rights results in total helplessness. However, though it underscores the need for human rights, the novel does not suggest how to achieve them. After all, once the animals expel Jones and gain rights for themselves, the pigs take those rights away and the cycle of exploitation continues with new players.

Apathy and Acceptance

In the beginning of *Animal Farm*, the idea of freedom rouses the animals as if from a long slumber. Immediately following Major's death, the animals begin preparing themselves for the Rebellion; just the idea of revolution is enough to motivate them, since they do not expect it to happen in their lifetimes. By the book's end, the animals have become as apathetic as Benjamin always was. Despite the many hardships and injustices they face, the animals' pride as well as Napoleon's propaganda keep them invested in the "greater good" and the illusion of freedom. If Benjamin is the harbinger of apathy, Boxer is its antithesis. Strong not only in body but also in spirit, Boxer will make any sacrifice for the benefit of Animal Farm. With Boxer's eventual betrayal by the leaders he served so unconditionally, Orwell lays bare another type of apathy—theirs. Far from truly considering Boxer a loyal comrade, the pigs treat him as apathetically as they would a mere object. Symbolically, they even make a profit by having him turned into literal objects—glue and bone meal.

Boxer's enthusiasm does not give him an advantage, but the other animals' eventual apathy gives them a defense mechanism against the painful reality of their lives. It is no coincidence that Animal Farm's most apathetic and cynical animal, Benjamin, is one of those that survives the longest. Benjamin's emotional detachment from situations, whether they are good or bad, keeps him from being disappointed. In his apathy and cynicism, Benjamin represents the stereotypical "gloomy" Russian and also the perennially pessimistic Orwell himself.

Glossary of Terms

coccidiosis

a parasitic infection that causes bloody diarrhea and sudden death in animals

communism

a theory or system of social organization based on the holding of all property in common, actual ownership being ascribed to the community as a whole or to the state; in practice, communism is often a totalitarian system of government

comrade

a fellow member of a political party; a member of the Communist party

disinter

to exhume; to unearth that which is buried

proletariat

in Marxism, the class of workers, especially industrial wage earners, who do not possess capital or property and must sell their labor to survive

propaganda

information, ideas, or rumors disseminated to help or harm a person, group, movement, institution, nation, or other entity

regime

a mode or system of rule or government; such a system when in power

socialism

a theory or system of social organization that advocates vesting the ownership and control of the means of production and distribution, of capital, land, and other assets in the community as a whole

totalitarianism

absolute control by the state or a governing branch of a highly centralized institution

tushes

small, short tusks such as those belonging to a boar

Short Summary

Animal Farm is a satirical fable set on Manor Farm, a typical English farm. Orwell employs a third-person narrator, who reports events without commenting on them directly. The narrator describes things as the animals perceive them.

Old Major calls a meeting of all the animals in the big barn. He announces that he may die soon and relates to them the insights he has gathered in his life. Old Major tells the animals that human beings are the sole reason that "No animal in England is free" and that "The life of an animal is misery and slavery." Therefore the animals must take charge of their destiny by overthrowing Man in a great Rebellion. He relates his dream of rebellion.

Old Major dies soon after the meeting and the other animals prepare for the Rebellion under Snowball, Napoleon, and Squealer's leadership. One night, Mr. Jones passes out drunk, creating the perfect opportunity for the animals to rebel. They are so hungry that they break into the store-shed. When Jones and his men try to whip them into submission, the animals run them off the farm. The animals burn all reminders of their former bondage but agree to preserve the farmhouse "as a museum." Snowball changes the name of the farm to "Animal Farm" and comes up with Seven Commandments, which are to form the basis of Animalism. They are:

1. Whatever goes upon two legs is an enemy.
2. Whatever goes upon four legs, or has wings, is a friend.
3. No animal shall wear clothes.
4. No animal shall sleep in a bed.
5. No animals shall drink alcohol.
6. No animal shall kill any other animal.
7. All animals are equal.

The pigs milk the cows, and then the animals go out to begin the harvest. When they return, the milk has disappeared mysteriously. The first harvest is a great success. The animals adhere to the tenets of Animalism happily, and with good result. Each animal works according to his ability and gets a fair share of food.

Every Sunday, Snowball and Napoleon lead a meeting of all the animals in the big barn. The pigs are the most intelligent animals, so they think up resolutions for the other animals to debate. Soon after, the pigs set up a study-center for themselves in the harness-room. Snowball embarks on various campaigns for social and economic improvement. Napoleon opposes whatever Snowball does. Because most of the animals lack the intelligence to memorize the Seven Commandments, Snowball reduces them to the single maxim, "Four legs good, two legs bad." The sheep take to chanting this at meetings.

As time goes by, the pigs increase their control over the animals and award themselves increasing privileges. They quell the animals' questions and protests by threatening Mr. Jones's return. During this time, Napoleon also confiscates nine newborn puppies and secludes them in a loft in order to "educate" them.

By late summer, Snowball's and Napoleon's pigeon-messengers have spread news of the Rebellion across half of England. Animals on other farms have begun lashing out against their human masters and singing the revolutionary song "Beasts of England." Jones and other farmers try to recapture Animal Farm but fail. The animals celebrate their victory in what they call "The Battle of the Cowshed."

The animals agree to let the pigs make all the resolutions. Snowball and Napoleon continue to be at odds and eventually clash over the windmill. Snowball wants to build a windmill in order to shorten the work week and provide the farm electricity, but Napoleon opposes it. Napoleon summons nine fierce dogs (the puppies he trained) to run Snowball off the farm. Napoleon announces that Sunday meetings will cease and that the pigs will make all the decisions in the animals' best interest. At this point, Boxer takes on his own personal maxims, "I will work harder" and "Napoleon is always right." In the spring, Napoleon announces plans to build the windmill, claiming that it was his idea all along—rewriting history.

Building the windmill forces the animals to work harder and on Sundays. Shortages begin to occur, so Napoleon opens up trade with the human world. Through Squealer, he lies that no resolutions against interaction with humans or the use of money had ever been passed. Napoleon enlists Whymper to be his intermediary, and the pigs move into the farmhouse. Squealer assures the animals that there is no resolution against this, but Clover and Muriel discovers that one of the resolutions has been changed to: "No animal shall sleep in a bed *with sheets*." Squealer convinces her that there was never a resolution against beds at all.

One night, strong winds shake the farm and the animals awake to discover the windmill destroyed. Napoleon blames Snowball and sentences the expelled pig to death.

In the winter, as conditions become worse on Animal Farm, Napoleon deceives the human world into thinking Animal Farm is prospering. He signs a contract for a quota of four hundred eggs per week, inciting a hen rebellion that results in several deaths. Around the same time, Napoleon begins negotiating with Frederick and Pilkington to sell Animal Farm's store of timber. He also spreads propaganda against Snowball, claiming that Snowball was always a spy and a collaborator while Napoleon was the true hero of the Battle of the Cowshed, and Squealer warns against Snowball's secret agents.

Four days later, Napoleon holds an assembly in which he makes several animals confess to treachery and then has the dogs execute them. The dogs try to get Boxer to confess but leave him alone when they cannot overpower him. Afterwards, Clover and some other animals huddle together on a hill overlooking the farm. They reminisce about Animalism's ideals and consider how much they differ from the violence and terror of Napoleon's reign. They sing "Beasts of England," but Squealer informs them that the song is useless now that the Rebellion is completed and that it is now forbidden. The new anthem begins with the lyrics: "Animal Farm, Animal Farm, / Never through me shalt thou come to harm!"

Another commandment is changed to read: "No animal shall kill any other animal *without cause*." Clover and Muriel convince themselves that the commandment has always been this way. Squealer begins reading the animals statistics regularly to convince them that production is increasing. Napoleon seldom appears in public. The animals now call him "our Leader, Comrade Napoleon." They attribute all misfortunes to Snowball and all success and luck to Napoleon.

Napoleon continues to negotiate with the farmers and eventually decides to sell the timber to Mr. Pilkington. At last, the windmill is finished and named "Napoleon Mill." Soon after, Napoleon announces that he will sell the timber to Frederick, quickly changing his allegiance and disavowing his earlier vilification of Frederick. Napoleon says that Pilkington and Snowball have been collaborating. Frederick pays for the timber in fake cash, and the next morning, Frederick and his men invade the farm and blow up the windmill. The animals manage to chase the humans off, though many die or are injured in what they call "The Battle of the Windmill."

After the battle, the pigs discover a case of whisky in the farmhouse. They drink to excess and soon, Squealer reports that Napoleon is dying and, as his last action, has made the consumption of alcohol punishable by death. But Napoleon recovers quickly and then sends Whymper to procure manuals on brewing alcohol. Squealer changes another commandment to "No animal shall drink alcohol *to excess*."

Napoleon plans to build a schoolhouse for the thirty-one young pigs he has parented. Towards the end of the winter, Napoleon begins increasing propaganda to distract the animals from inequality and hardship. He creates special "Spontaneous Demonstrations" in which the animals march around and celebrate their triumphs.

In April, Napoleon declares the farm a Republic and is elected unanimously as President. The animals continue to work feverishly, most of all Boxer. One day, Boxer collapses while overexerting himself. Napoleon promises to send him to the veterinarian in Willingdon. A few days later, a horse-slaughterer takes Boxer away in his van. The animals are none the wiser until Benjamin reads the lettering on the side of the van. A few days later, Squealer reports that Boxer died in the hospital despite receiving the best possible care. He claims that Boxer's last words glorified Animal Farm and Napoleon. He also claims that the van belongs to the veterinarian, who recently bought it from the horse slaughterer and had not yet managed to paint over the lettering. Napoleon promises to honor Boxer with a special banquet. But the pigs use the money from his slaughter to buy a case of whisky, which they drink on the day appointed for the banquet.

Years go by, and though Animal Farm's population has increased, only a few animals that remember the Rebellion remain. Conditions are still harsh despite technological improvements. The pigs and dogs continue to do no manual labor, instead devoting themselves to organizational work. One day, Squealer takes the sheep out to a deserted pasture where, he says, he is teaching them a song. On the day the sheep return, the pigs walk around the yard on their hind legs as the sheep chant, "Four legs good, two legs *better*." The other animals are horrified. Clover consults the barn wall again. This time Benjamin reads to her. The Seven Commandments have been replaced with a single maxim: "All animals are equal / But some animals are more equal than others."

The pigs continue the longstanding pattern of awarding themselves more and more privileges. They buy a telephone and subscribe to magazines. They even wear Jones's clothing. One night, Napoleon holds a conciliatory banquet for the farmers. Pilkington makes a speech in which he says he wants to emulate Animal Farm's long work hours and low rations. Napoleon announces that the farm will be called "Manor Farm" again, the animals will call each other "Comrade" no longer, and they no longer will march ceremoniously past Old Major's skull (a practice he denies understanding). He also declares that the farm's flag will be plain green, devoid of the symbols of the Rebellion. As the animals peer through the windows to watch the humans and pigs play poker, they cannot distinguish between them.

Summary and Analysis of Chapter I

Mr. Jones, the owner of Manor Farm, stumbles drunkenly up to bed as the farm animals wait in still silence. The moment he is out of sight, they begin to bustle around, preparing themselves for the big meeting that is to take place that night. Old Major has called the meeting to discuss a strange dream he had the previous night. He is waiting for his fellow animals in the big barn.

The first animals to arrive are the three dogs, Bluebell, Jessie, and Pincher, followed by the pigs. Hens, pigeons, sheep, and cows arrive, as well as the horses, Boxer and Clover. Muriel, the white goat, and the donkey Benjamin follow. A group of motherless ducklings wanders in and Clover, being the motherly type, forms a safe place for them to sit with her leg. Mollie, the young mare, arrives just before the cat, who settles in between Boxer and Clover. The only animal missing is Moses, the raven, who is sleeping on his perch behind the barn door.

Old Major addresses the animals, calling them, "Comrades." He explains that, because he is getting old and may die soon, he wishes to impart his wisdom. Over his lifetime, he has come to the conclusions that "No animal in England is free" and "The life of an animal is misery and slavery" (28).

Old Major states that animals' domination by Man is the sole reason they cannot be free, happy, and fulfilled. Man is "the only creature that consumes without producing." His only job is to be "lord of all the animals," which makes him "the only real enemy" animals have. Man overworks animals only to rob them of the fruits of their labor, and treats them only well enough to survive and provide more labor. When Man is done with an animal, he slaughters it cruelly.

According to Old Major, Rebellion is the path to freedom. Overthrowing the human race would make animals "rich and free" almost instantly. Old Major begs the other animals to devote the rest of their lives to the cause of Rebellion and to reject the idea that they have co-dependence with Man. Furthermore, the animals must be united in order to overthrow man: "All men are enemies. All animals are comrades" (31). Despite this saying, he is not sure whether wild animals count.

Old Major holds a vote to decide whether domesticated animals should unite with wild animals. Only the dogs and the cat vote no, although the cat is not paying attention and votes twice. After the vote, Old Major crystallizes his point, stating: "Whatever goes upon two legs is an enemy. Whatever goes upon four legs, or has wings, is a friend." He adds the additional point that, once they have achieved victory, animals must not emulate Man. They must not wear clothing, live in houses, or copy any of Man's other "evil" habits.

Finally, Old Major relates his dream to the animals. His dream was about the state of happiness that will exist once Man is eliminated. In the dream, a tune his mother and the other sows sang to him in his childhood returned to him, and new words accompanied the tune. Old Major is sure that he has, in his dream life, uncovered an old animal anthem that has lain dormant for generations. It is called "Beasts of England," and he sings it to the other animals. Orwell describes the song as "a stirring tune, something between Clementine and La Cucaracha" (32). The song glorifies the freedom and joy that will follow "Tyrant Man's" overthrow, and he urges all animals to "toil for freedom's sake," even if they die before the cause is won.

The song rouses the animals, even the dullest of whom learn it in minutes. In fact, the animals are so taken with the song that they sing it five times in unison. The ruckus awakes Mr. Jones, who fires several bullets from his shotgun into the barn wall. The animals rush to their sleeping places, and the farm is silent once again.

Analysis

Chapter I introduces us to the idealism upon which Animal Farm and Animalism will later be built. In explicating Animal Farm, some critics stress Orwell's broad focus on totalitarianism over his specific criticism of Stalinism. After all, Orwell saw the threat of totalitarianism (and elitism) manifested not only in Soviet Russia but also in places such as Spain and colonial Britain. However, despite Animal Farm's far political reach, Orwell did write it as a cautionary tale about Stalinism specifically and, as we shall see, matched its plot quite closely with Russian history. We can read the novel as both a specific and a general allegory.

Old Major assumes the role of philosopher, creating a detailed model for a utopian society. His role is also that of visionary or prophet because, smart as he is, part of Major's vision of the future came to him in a dream. In his roles of philosopher and visionary, Major represents the political theorist Karl Marx. Old Major is older and wiser than the other animals, a fact that mirrors history. Marx and his theories predated (and therefore influenced) the ideas of Lenin, Trotsky, and Stalin. All three men were still children at the time of Marx's death.

Major's vision of mankind's problems and his plan for a utopian society closely match the tenets of Marxism as expressed in The Communist Manifesto. Major's ideas of the animal and Man correspond with Marx's views of the common man and the elite. We should bear this symbolism in mind as we examine Major's speech. First, Old Major focuses on the exploitation of the animal by Man, who is concerned only with making a profit. Although the animal does all the work, it gets no stake in what it produces because man controls not only the means of production but also the means of distribution. Marxism argues that the common man becomes confused by the elite's self-serving ideology and becomes separated from its true nature. In the same way, Major says that Man keeps animals in submission only because he is the one creating the ideology and the rules. In order to claim their destiny of being "rich and free," the animals must overthrow Man.

Major also represents Vladimir Lenin, the foremost author of the Russian Revolution and of the formation of the Soviet Union. If historically Marx played the role of grandfather theorist, then Lenin played that of young interpreter and motivator. Old Major not only bestows his theory upon the animals, he awakens them from the dreamtime of Man's ideology and rouses them to action. He does so with the help of "Beasts of England," a revolutionary song that helps the animals envision the "golden future time" when they will live free of man's (literal and metaphorical) yoke. Orwell also connects Major to Lenin by his use of the word "comrade," which is associated with communism.

If Major represents Marx and Lenin, two revolutionary forces, then Jones represents the existing totalitarian regime. He symbolizes imperial Russia and the ineffective Czar Nicholas II. Jones stands for an ideology and methodology that have been in practice for a very long time. In all the history of Manor Farm, the animals have never risen up against him nor thought of doing so. Though they are superior in numbers and strength, they cannot match his intellectual capabilities (or at least think they cannot). We should also note that Moses the raven is Jones's "especial pet." Moses represents the religion that, in the Russian Empire, was connected closely with the throne. Jones feeds Moses bread soaked in beer to keep him tame, just as the Russian throne cooperated with the Church but kept it on a tight leash. Under Marxism-Leninism, religion is one of the things that appeases the common man and makes him easier to subjugate; as Marx famously stated, "religion is the opiate of the masses." It has no value in a truly utopian society, such theorists believe, because people are satisfied in reality and no longer feel the need to rely on faith or the promise of heaven. It follows that Moses is conspicuously absent from Major's big meeting.

Summary and Analysis of Chapter II

Old Major dies three nights after the meeting that united the animals. Over the next three months, the more intelligent animals begin to approach life differently. They now anticipate the Rebellion, for which they assume the task of preparing. The pigs take on the task of organizing and teaching the other animals because they are "generally recognized as being the cleverest of the animals" (35).

Snowball, Napoleon, and Squealer have taken charge especially, and they have expanded Old Major's concept into a "complete system of thought" called Animalism. They hold frequent meetings in the big barn to espouse the views of Animalism to the other farm animals. At first, the animals are not convinced that they should follow Animalism. Some feel loyalty to Mr. Jones, some worry that they cannot be self-sufficient, and others, such as Mollie, worry about losing treats such as sugar and ribbons. Snowball contradicts Mollie, saying that the ribbons are "the badge of slavery" and that "liberty is worth more than ribbons" (37).

Moses causes trouble for the pigs by inventing an animal heaven called Sugarcandy Mountain., a utopia for another time. In contrast, Clover and Boxer are some of the pigs' strongest collaborators. Not being very intelligent themselves, Clover and Boxer memorize simple pro-Animalism arguments that they pass on to the others.

Monetary troubles plague Mr. Jones, leading him to drink excessively. The farmhands are lazy and fail to tend the farm well, yet hard times for Mr. Jones mean a leg up for the animals. In fact, Mr. Jones's misfortune makes the Rebellion come earlier than expected. On Midsummer's Eve in June, Mr. Jones gets so drunk that he passes out and neglects to feed the animals. Having gone unfed for hours, the animals break into the store-shed and eat. Mr. Jones and the farmhands rush in and begin whipping the animals indiscriminately, and the animals respond by attacking them in unison. The men are frightened and forced to flee the farm.

After a disbelieving calm, the animals barge into the harness-room and drown or burn all the implements of their former bondage. Snowball makes sure to burn the ribbons, which he calls tantamount to clothing, and states, "All animals should go naked" (40). The animals then help themselves to double servings of food and sleep better than they ever have. When they awake the next morning, they survey the farm with new eyes, absorbing the fact that it is now their own. Finally, they tour the farmhouse, seeing in disbelief the "unbelievable luxury" in which the Joneses had lived. Then the animals agree to leave the farmhouse intact as a museum. They confiscate a few hams for burial and leave.

The pigs reveal that they have taught themselves to read and write from an old children's book, which they burned in the bonfire of human belongings. Snowball uses paint to replace the title "Manor Farm" with "Animal Farm" on the farm gate. Back in the big barn, they reveal that they have reduced Animalism to Seven

Commandments. The animals must live by these commandments "for ever after." The commandments, which Snowball writes on the wall with some typographical errors, are:

1. Whatever goes upon two legs is an enemy.
2. Whatever goes upon four legs, or has wings, is a friend.
3. No animal shall wear clothes.
4. No animal shall sleep in a bed.
5. No animal shall drink alcohol.
6. No animal shall kill any other animal.
7. All animals are equal.

After reading the Seven Commandments out loud, Snowball declares that the animals must begin the hay harvest. Three cows interrupt his thought by lowing in pain, since their udders are full to bursting. Some pigs milk the cows, producing "five buckets of frothing creamy milk" (44). The animals wonder what to do with the milk, but Napoleon puts off that decision for a later time. The animals begin the harvest in the fields, and when they return the milk is gone.

Analysis

Old Major's death represents Lenin's death in 1924, which left Stalin (Napoleon) and Trotsky (Snowball) to vie for the leadership position. Major's meeting changes the animals' outlook on life, but Orwell is careful to mention that not all the animals quite grasp Major's idea of a utopian society. All the animals can learn "Beasts of England," but only those smart enough can truly assume the revolutionary spirit and the task of preparing for the Rebellion. The pigs become the organizers very quickly. It is important to note two things about their rise to power. First, the pigs have not always been in charge of the other animals, though later in the book when the pigs are so thoroughly demonized, Orwell makes it hard for the animals—and the reader—to remember that. But they are superior by nature—or at least by tradition—when it comes to intelligence. Second, the pigs' intentions are not necessarily bad at first. They take on the task of organization because of their reputed superiority rather than a desire to take control for themselves. Just as Boxer is best suited for hard manual labor, the pigs take their place for organizational work in the animals' division of labor.

Snowball, Napoleon, and Squealer organize Major's ideas into the theory of Animalism, which can stand for any "complete system of thought" but is meant to evoke Soviet Communism. If Snowball and Napoleon represent the organizers of Communism, then the other pigs represent those of the Russian intelligentsia who became involved in the revolutionary cause. The Seven Commandments represent Communism in its theoretical, idealized form. In writing, the Seven Commandments look fair and hold true to Major's stipulation that the animals not emulate humans. Though the animals intend to live by the Seven Commandments "for ever after," we will learn quickly that the tenets of Animalism do not translate perfectly into reality, especially not with the seeds of elitism already planted among the pigs.

Like any new theory, Animalism is met with doubt and opposition. The most notable objection comes from Mollie, the fickle mare that represents Russia's elite. Although the common animals also doubt Animalism, Mollie is spoiled by the special treatment she received under Jones's rule (mirroring the czar's rule). She also, despite being superficial and fickle, has the intelligence and the resources to get herself out of Animal Farm, which the "peasant" animals lack. Historically, many of the Russian elite were unwilling to give up their privileges, just as Mollie is loath to give up ribbons, sugar, or being petted. Like Mollie, they became expatriates in capitalist societies where they could retain their advantages (this was a particularly wise move, considering what had happened to the nobility during the French Revolution). Moses also presents a challenge to Animalism, just as religion presented a challenge to Communism. Historically, Stalin used intimidation and force to crush religion and promote atheism in the Soviet Union. However, despite their efforts to promote their ideas over those of Moses, the leadership of Animal Farm allows Moses to come and go as he pleases. The struggles and inconsistencies of Animalism as practiced can be made softer by belief in an animal heaven to be enjoyed later.

Mr. Jones's monetary troubles mirror the Russian throne's ineffectiveness and dwindling power on the eve of the Revolution. The air is ripe for revolution, and the animals seize the opportunity to run Jones off his own land. The animals are kinder to Jones than the revolutionaries were to Czar Nicholas II, who was executed on Lenin's orders along with his family.

With Jones gone, the animals begin to realize Major's vision of a utopian, animal-run society that operates under its own ideology. The Rebellion could represent the February Revolution (though it happens on Midsummer's Eve) or the Russian Revolution as a whole. The February Revolution did result in Czar Nicholas II's abdication, which Jones's expulsion mirrors neatly. The story, however, does not need a one-to-one correspondence with history, and Orwell can make his points more crisply by adapting the history to his carefully crafted allegory.

Although the animals live happily for a while, it is important to note that the pigs have begun their clandestine and elitist activities already. For example, they order that all artifacts of the animals' oppression be burned. The pigs thus burn a children's book they used to teach themselves to read and write, but the resource is no longer available after the book-burning. Throughout the novel, Orwell emphasizes the other animals' lack of intelligence, but we can never be sure that the animals' ignorance and illiteracy is due to lack of intelligence rather than an oppressive environment, generation after generation, that has made their lower status and ability seem natural. When the pigs take the milk for themselves, the reader knows that this is the beginning of a new round of subjugation and oppression by an elite.

Summary and Analysis of Chapter III

The harvest is more of a success than Mr. Jones and his men ever accomplished, despite the fact that the tools are not well suited for animals to use, especially without the animals rearing up on their hind legs. The pigs supervise the others but do not participate in the manual labor. With the "parasitical human beings" out of the way, the animals enjoy a feeling of abundance for the first time. They have more leisure, and their food tastes all the better for their having gathered and portioned it out themselves.

On Animal Farm, everyone works "according to his capacity." Boxer is invigorated and pushes himself to work harder than ever; because he is strong and big, he contributes to the most strenuous labor. In contrast, the hens and ducks work at gathering small bits of corn that the bigger animals would not be able to gather. The system of Animalism is working well: every animal is satisfied with his share of the labor and its fruits. No one steals or argues, and very few shirk their responsibilities, with the exception of the cat and frivolous Mollie.

Every Sunday is a day of rest and devotion to Animalism on Animal Farm. The animals hold an hour-long ceremony at which they raise their new flag. The flag is green to represent England's pastures and features a hoof and horn that "represent the future Republic of the Animals" that will exist "when the human race [has] finally been overthrown" (48). A gathering called Meeting follows the flag raising, in which the animals plan the coming week and the pigs present resolutions for debate (none of the other animals are intelligent enough to think up resolutions). Snowball and Napoleon tend to debate the most and take opposite sides. The animals end each meeting by singing "Beasts of England."

The pigs set up a study center for themselves in the harness-room, where they study trades using Mr. Jones's books. Snowball begins organizing the animals into Animal Committees, including the Egg Production Committee, the Clean Tails League, the Wild Comrades' Re-education Committee (to tame rats and rabbits), and the Whiter Wool Movement. These committees generally fail to produce results or remain cohesive. Snowball does succeed in teaching some of the animals to read, although most of them lack the intelligence needed for literacy. In fact, many of the animals lack the intelligence needed to memorize the Seven Commandments, so Snowball reduces Animalism's tenets to one simple saying: "Four legs good, two legs bad" (50).

As time goes by, the pigs begin to increase their control over the other animals. For example, when Jessie and Bluebell give birth to puppies, Napoleon takes them to an isolated loft where he can teach them. Napoleon believes that educating young, impressionable animals is more important than trying to re-educate older ones. It turns out that the pigs are mixing the cows' milk with their food. When the wind knocks ripe apples out of the orchard trees, the pigs claim the right to take them all, as well as the bulk of the coming apple harvest. The pigs claim that they need milk and apples in order to power their "brainwork." Squealer says that, were the pigs to stop eating milk and apples, they could lose their powers of organization and Mr. Jones could come back. The threat of Mr. Jones's return is enough to quell the other animals' doubts and questions.

Analysis

At first, the animals seem to be living in the utopia Major had imagined for them. Now that they have their own ideology and own the means of production, they feel "rich and free," just as Major predicted. They enjoy a temporary calm as well as a sense of invigoration after years of discontent, now assume Man's position of control over themselves and nature. In doing organizational work, the pigs are working in accordance with their capacity. But at the same time, the pigs are fairly large and strong animals that could surely contribute to the farm's manual labor force. They are slowly assuming Man's competitive advantage and becoming "the only creature that consumes without producing."

From the very beginning of the Animal Farm era, Boxer assumes the majority of the burden of labor. Now that he is working for the animals' benefit and not Jones's, he feels enlivened and adopts the first of his two personal maxims, "I will work harder." In his heartiness, usefulness, and relative dullness, Boxer represents the faithful peasant. Some critics have pointed out the similarity of this motto to that of the main character in Upton Sinclair's The Jungle. Indeed, Orwell was certainly familiar with Sinclair's writings. While Sinclair's novel criticized capitalism, Orwell's focuses on Communism. Either way, the point expands the reader's consciousness to see how elitism can result in willing subjugation in very different regimes. Boxer is not pugnacious despite his name, but he is as strong as his name implies. In this way, Boxer is painfully ironic. He is strong enough to kill another animal, even a human, with a single blow from his hoof, and the dogs will not be able to overpower him in Chapter VII. Still, Boxer lacks the intelligence and the nerve to sense that he is being misled and mistreated. He knows how to use his brawn only in submission to his leaders and not against them.

Chapter III marks the beginning of the dispute between Snowball and Napoleon, which evokes the power struggle between Trotsky and Stalin. After Trotsky's fashion, Snowball is a progressive, eloquent, and public politician. He not only creates countless plans for reform, but he also dominates the Sunday meetings with his skillful and rabble-rousing orations. Snowball has the capacity to inspire the animals just as Major did in his big meeting. After Stalin's fashion, Napoleon conducts his politics clandestinely. His public statements are generally limited to rebuttals of Snowball's ideas; he keeps his own plans to himself. For example, Napoleon secrets the puppies away to a loft and, by keeping out of the public eye, manages to rear them into fierce, blood-hungry, creatures submissive to him. Napoleon's collaboration with and control of the dogs evokes Stalin's focus on quietly gaining support from powerful allies.

Chapter III also introduces the idea of propaganda. "Stirring" as it may be, "Beasts of England" is more of a revolutionary anthem than a piece of propaganda. It is meant to unite the animals in the cause of the Rebellion and help them to envision the utopia for which they must strive. But most of the animals are not intelligent enough to let the song do more than vaguely inspire their hopes. Without even being able to remember the Seven Commandments, most of the animals rely merely on the propagandist refrain, "Four legs good, two legs bad." Snowball reduces the Seven Commandments into this single maxim, vastly oversimplifying the full system of Animalism into a catchphrase. As the animals adopt the phrase, they begin to forget the Seven Commandments, which gives the pigs the opportunity to change them. In fact, the pigs manage to break every one of the other commandments without arousing much suspicion. Clover and Muriel, who periodically think about the Seven Commandments, are easily duped in this regard. Having memorized the simple maxim in their place, they are easily convinced that their doubts about the original content of the commandments are unfounded.

Squealer, who represents the propaganda machine, introduces fear tactics in this chapter. After convincing the animals that the pigs have a right to milk and apples, he threatens the animals with Jones's return for the first time. The pigs have created an environment where their rules must be followed out of fear of the return of the old older. It is an easy, winning response to animals that see only the two alternatives and cannot see a way back to the utopian principles that inspired their rebellion.

Summary and Analysis of Chapter IV

It is late summer. News of the Rebellion has spread to many other farms, thanks to Snowball's and Napoleon's pigeon messengers. Meanwhile, in the human world, Mr. Jones tells other farmers about the Rebellion. The fear of similar revolutions unites the owners of the farms adjacent to Animal Farm, even though they dislike one another. Easy-going Mr. Pilkington (of large, neglected Foxwood) and hard-nosed Mr. Frederick (of small, better-kept Pinchfield) spread rumors to discourage their animals from turning against them. They say that the animals on Manor Farm are starving. When this claim turns out to be clearly untrue, they claim that the animals are cannibals who practice all kinds of wickedness.

Despite the farmers' efforts to subdue ideas of rebellion, their animals begin lashing out against them. The animals resist the farmers' orders. They also adopt the infuriating habit of singing "Beasts of England."

In October, accompanied by several other farmers, Mr. Jones tries to recapture Animal Farm. Snowball has already trained the animals for war, however, and they take their defensive positions. The smaller animals attack the men and then pretend to retreat into the yard in defeat. Once the men follow, the larger animals ambush them. Mr. Jones kills one sheep and wounds Snowball several times with his gun, but the animals manage to overpower the humans. Boxer is thought to have killed a stable-lad, which upsets the stalwart horse. But it turns out that the boy is only injured, and he flees with the other men. The only animal who does not fight is Mollie, whom the animals discover cowering in her stall.

After the battle, the animals sing "Beasts of England" yet again. They invent a military honor called "Animal Hero, First Class," which they bestow upon Snowball and Boxer. Then they bury the fallen sheep and confer upon him posthumously the title of "Animal Hero, Second Class." The animals decide to call this conflict the Battle of the Cowshed. The agree to fire Mr. Jones's gun into the air twice a year, on the anniversaries of the battle (October 12) and of the Rebellion (Midsummer's Eve).

Analysis

The first part of Chapter IV mirrors the international reaction to the young Soviet Union. For centuries, other nations had been able to write off Russia as a backwards and disorganized country, despite the size of its territory and population. There had been socialist uprisings elsewhere, and efforts like the French Revolution had not brought the workers' utopia that had been dreamed of. But after the Russian Revolution, and armed with a new ideology and power structure, the Soviet Union began to garner international interest due to its prospects for success. Communism thus re-entered the realm of international politics as a possibly viable alternative to fascism and capitalism, and workers around the world were hopeful that the promises of the Soviets would come to fruition everywhere. We see this history reflected in the farmers' growing awareness of the happenings on Animal Farm and in the animals' rebelliousness on their own farms.

Part of Trotsky's politics (called Trotskyism) was the belief that the Revolution should be encouraged in other countries, leading to an international revolution of the proletariat. Orwell mirrors this view in Snowball's pigeon-messenger missions; he enlists the birds to spread news of the Rebellion to farms across England. Thus, Animal Farm is not just an example of change but an agent of the new solidarity of the animals.

Snowball's efforts work to an extent, since animals on other farms not only start disobeying their owners but also agitate the owners--as Trotsky's ideas agitated foreign nations. At once fascinated and threatened by the Soviets' increasing power, some foreign leaders found the need to suppress the seeds of revolution in their own countries. Thus, when Pilkington and Frederick spread lies about Animal Farm, they represent the Western vilification of Communism. Although the farmers and capitalists to some degree were just protecting their own investments, it turns out that the villains really are the pigs and the Stalinists after all.

Jones's attempt to recapture Animal Farm strengthens the bonds between the animals. The animals, small and large, work together to successfully overthrow the humans once more. Of course, the animals do not like the war. At the same time, it strengthens their determination to maintain their freedom and work for the greater good.

The Battle of the Cowshed also creates a legend about Snowball's heroism that will become subject to revisionism throughout the book. In truth, Snowball leads the charge against Jones and his men, being shot several times in the process. Over time, memories will fade and the battle will be reinterpreted by those in power.

According to some critics, the Battle of the Cowshed represents the October Revolution, in which the Bolsheviks replaced the provisional government. This idea is supported by the battle's date (October 12) and the animals' post-battle resolution to fire the gun on the anniversaries of the Rebellion and the Battle of the Cowshed; in that resolution, Orwell seems to liken the two events to two main turns in the Russian Revolution. But Orwell does not give us a neat parallel with history. Russia was disorganized and dissatisfied under the provisional government, whereas Animal Farm is already prospering in Chapter IV. Also, the animals are already living by the Seven Commandments, which symbolize the Soviet decrees passed after the October Revolution. As we will see in the refiguring of the Red Terror, Orwell does not adhere tightly to historical progression in the novel, letting his own message take precedence.

Summary and Analysis of Chapter V

As winter approaches, Mollie's behavior becomes increasingly perturbed. She is late for work and feigns injury in order to shirk her duties. More seriously, Clover has spotted Mollie at the border of Foxwood, allowing Mr. Pilkington to stroke her nose and talk to her. Mollie denies the accusation, but her embarrassment confirms that she is lying. On a hunch, Clover goes to Mollie's stall and finds a hidden stash of sugar and ribbons. Mollie disappears soon after. She is seen in a painted cart, gussied up and taking sugar from a man who appears to be some kind of manager. The other animals never mention her again.

January brings bitterly cold weather. Since conditions are too harsh for farming, the animals hold many meetings. They have agreed that the pigs should make all policy decisions, which the other animals are to ratify. Snowball and Napoleon are in constant disagreement, and the other animals begin to take sides. The sheep support Napoleon and interrupt Snowball's speeches by bleating, "Four legs good, two legs bad." Snowball is the more progressive politician, promoting innovations to make the farm run more efficiently. Napoleon makes sure to oppose all of Snowball's ideas.

After some time, Snowball and Napoleon come into bitter conflict over a windmill. Snowball designates a piece of land for a windmill, which will provide electricity for the heretofore-primitive farm. He uses Mr. Jones's books to draft a detailed chalk blueprint, which fascinates the other animals. One day, Napoleon urinates on the blueprint to show his disdain.

Snowball estimates that the animals can complete the windmill with a year of hard labor, after which the time saving machine will shorten their workweek to three days. Napoleon counters with the idea that they will all starve to death in that time, and that the farm's primary concern should be increasing food production. The animals split into two groups, one called "Vote for Snowball and the three-day week," the other called "Vote for Napoleon and the full manger" (65). The only animal not to take a side is Benjamin, who is pessimistic about both plans.

Snowball and Napoleon engage in another major debate about how best to prepare for another human attack. Napoleon advocates the procurement of firearms as well as firearms training. Snowball advocates sending pigeons to rally the other animals; if rebellions occur everywhere, then the humans will stay at bay. The other animals do not divide over this issue because they cannot decide who is right.

Finally, Snowball completes his blueprint for the windmill. The animals hold a meeting at which Snowball wins over the majority with his descriptions of the leisurely life that the windmill will allow. Suddenly, Napoleon signals "nine enormous dogs wearing brass-studded collars," which barge into the barn and chase Snowball out. Snowball manages to escape through a hedge. The frightened animals gather once more in the barn. As it turns out, the nine dogs are Jessie's and Bluebell's puppies. They seem to consider Napoleon their master. Napoleon takes the stage and announces that Sunday meetings with all their accompanying debates will cease, and he will lead a small committee of pigs in making decisions. This mandate disturbs the other animals, but most of them are too dull to argue and too afraid of the dogs to show their disapproval. Four pigs protest briefly.

After the meeting, Squealer explains the new arrangement to the other animals. Just as in the case of the milk and apples, Squealer claims that taking on leadership responsibilities is a burden for Napoleon and his committee; they do it only for the general welfare. If left to make their own decisions, he explains, the animals might make a wrong decision. He also calls Snowball a criminal; even if he was brave in the Battle of the Cowshed (an idea that Squealer also questions), "loyalty and obedience are more important." Squealer tells the animals, "Discipline, comrades, iron discipline! That is the watchword for today." Again as in the case of the milk and apples, Squealer ensures the animals' compliance by threatening Mr. Jones's return. Of all the animals, Boxer takes obedience to the pigs to heart most. He now has two personal maxims: "Napoleon is always right" and "I will work harder" (70).

Winter turns into spring. The pigs disinter Old Major's skull and place it at the base of the flagpole beside the gun. When they meet to receive their orders for the week, the animals no longer sit all together. Rather, the dogs and other pigs gather around Napoleon, Squealer, and another pig named Minimus. Only three days after Snowball's removal, Napoleon announces plans to build the windmill and make similar improvements to the farm. Squealer explains to the animals that Napoleon had never really opposed the windmill—in fact, it was "his own creation," which Snowball had copied. With evident pride, Squealer explains that Napoleon's feigned opposition to the windmill was simply a "maneuver" in his plan to expel Snowball for disobedience; it was a brilliant example of "tactics" (72).

Analysis

In Chapter IV, we saw conflicting evidence concerning the relationship between the Battle of the Cowshed and the historical October Revolution. Mollie's desertion in the beginning of Chapter V makes a case for the Battle of the Cowshed's representing the October Revolution. Once both parts of the Russian Revolution were completed (insofar as these were two touchstones of the revolution), Lenin could begin making major social and economic changes. Again, many improvements have already been instated on Animal Farm by the time of the Battle of the Cowshed, which would be too early for consistency with history—but not necessarily out of order for Marxist theory. If the trend toward collectivization after the Rebellion ruffled Mollie, the second revolutionary struggle, the Battle of the Cowshed, incites her to action. Just as many of Russia's former elite emigrated after the Russian Revolution because they refused to live under Communism, Mollie "emigrates" in order to avoid living under Animalism. The fact that Mollie leaves only after the Battle of the Cowshed supports its representing the October Revolution.

After the Battle of the Cowshed, the pigs award themselves the task or "burden" of making all policy decisions. This fact also supports the idea that the Battle of the Cowshed represents the October Revolution because, although the Seven Commandments are already in place, the pigs tighten their control over the populace just as the Bolsheviks did once the Revolution was complete. In general, Chapter V corresponds to the mid-to-late 1920s, when Trotsky and Stalin's power struggle came to a head. Historically, Trotsky was a brilliant orator, so he was good at inspiring the public on a large scale. Orwell mirrors this in the faction called "Vote for Napoleon and the three-day week." However, Stalin easily outdid Trotsky in his ability to garner not just a wash of support, but deep-seated and influential support. Snowball may dominate the stage at meetings, but Napoleon gets the sheep to heckle Snowball by interrupting his speeches by chanting, "Four legs good, two legs bad!" In their heckling, the sheep represent those of Stalin's supporters who took to disrupting Trotsky's speeches at Party meetings.

Orwell does not have a literary reason to follow the details of history and character because he is doing much more than retell a story in his own way; he chooses his details and his symbols in order to make his own points. The windmill is at the center of Snowball's and Napoleon's fiercest debate. Rather than representing a specific point of debate between Trotsky and Stalin, the windmill symbolizes Soviet industry, both agricultural and factory. The narrator tells us that, up until the building of the windmill, Manor Farm has been stuck in the past. It is not technologically advanced, though other farms are. This mirrors the fact that, coming into the Soviet Era, Russia's agriculture and city industry lagged behind other civilized countries. All of the three original Soviet leaders, Lenin, Trotsky, and Stalin, recognized the need for industrial progress and had varying ideas about how to pursue it. In his conception and promotion of the windmill, Snowball can be seen to take a turn as Lenin. Lenin's New Economic Policy (NEP) was an attempt to stimulate Russian productivity, one that Stalin ceased and replaced with his own "windmills," the Five Year Plans. On a broader scale, the windmill represents the abstract Soviet cause toward the common good.

Over the years, the animals will work tirelessly to build the windmill, sacrificing everything from their rest days to their rations in order that it might be completed. In the same way, Soviet citizens labored for an abstract "common good," the fruits of which they never saw. Each time the windmill is destroyed, Napoleon gives the animals new hope that, next time around, they will build it and reap its benefits. In the same way, Stalin kept the Soviet people trained on a good that, time after time, slipped from their grasp.

In Chapter V, Orwell also brings up the central difference between Trotskyism and Stalinism. As we have discussed previously, Trotsky advocated the extension of the Revolution on an international scale. In contrast, Stalin advanced the idea of Socialism in One Country, in which he stated that, considering the failure of communism in other nations, the Soviet Union should focus its energy internally. Stalin's Socialism in One Country was a revision of Marxism-Leninism. Orwell mirrors these events in Snowball's and Napoleon's debate over how best to protect Animal Farm against another human attack. Snowball wants to send messengers to spread the message of the Rebellion. Napoleon wants to stockpile weapons and train the animals to use them. Just as Stalin revised Marxism-Leninism with Socialism in One Country, Napoleon has begun to hijack Animalism to serve his own ideals.

In 1929, Stalin expelled Trotsky from the Soviet Union. In a similar move, Napoleon ousts Snowball from Animal Farm. Snowball's rabble-rousing cannot protect him against Napoleon's dogs, just as Trotsky's oration skills were no match for the power that Stalin was slowly and steadily cultivating. The revelation of the attack dogs is the first sign of the new violence between animals on Animal Farm. It is a kind of coup.

Under Napoleon, as under Stalin, propaganda takes on a much-expanded and more powerful role. Specifically, Squealer comes to represent Stalin's revisionist propaganda machine. No sooner than Snowball is gone, Squealer is already questioning Snowball's bravery in the Battle of the Cowshed. Notably, Squealer claims that the windmill was Napoleon's idea all along. Whether this is true or not, it certainly seems like revisionist history.

With the exhumation of old Major's skull, Orwell makes the point that propaganda is often effective not simply for its message but for the atmosphere of domination it creates. Napoleon is changing Major's ideas in order to create his own personal regime in the same way that Stalin changed Marxism-Leninism. Still, he makes the animals march past Major's skull as though they are still adhering to the old boar's exhortations.

Summary and Analysis of Chapter VI

The animals work sixty-hour weeks all spring and summer in order to build the windmill, but none begrudges the extra labor. In August, Napoleon instates "strictly voluntary" labor on Sundays: animals may choose not to come, but they will have their rations reduced by half. There are plenty of building materials on the premises, and the animals discover that they can break limestone into pieces by using the force of gravity. However, the process of dragging boulders to the top of the quarry and throwing them down is very taxing. Boxer compensates by picking up the other animals' slack, for which they admire him.

Shortages begin to occur. The animals require things, such as iron for horseshoes and machinery for the windmill, that they cannot produce on the farm. To provide a solution, Napoleon opens trade with the neighboring farms and says that the animals may need to sell some of the hens' eggs in the nearby town of Willingdon. He makes sure to stress the fact that the windmill should be the animals' first priority. The other animals are "conscious of a vague uneasiness" because the Seven Commandments forbid trade with humans and the use of money. Napoleon assures the animals that they, at least, will not have to make contact with human beings. He has already set up an agreement with a solicitor in town named Mr. Whymper, who will act as their intermediary to the human world.

After the meeting, Squealer assures the animals that trade and the use of money are allowed after all—that no resolution against those activities has ever been passed. He convinces them that their memory of such a resolution is mistaken. Mr. Whymper visits the farm every Monday to get his orders. Meanwhile, in the human world, humans are more opposed than ever to Animal Farm's existence. They hope that the windmill will fail and the farm will go bankrupt. Still, they secretly admire Animal Farm's efficiency, which they have begun to call by its new name. They even stop valorizing Mr. Jones, who has moved away.

One day, the pigs move into the farmhouse. The other animals again feel uneasy, remembering faintly a resolution that forbade such an action. Again, Squealer convinces them that they are mistaken. Napoleon, whom Squealer now calls "The Leader," should be granted the honor of living in a house. Furthermore, the pigs need a quiet workplace. Squealer's lies satisfy some of the animals. But Clover decides to investigate when she learns that the pigs have taken to sleeping in beds. She tries to read the Seven Commandments on the barn wall, but she cannot. Muriel is able to read it for her. One resolution has been changed to: "No animal shall sleep in a bed with sheets" (79). At this point, Squealer approaches and denies that there was ever a rule against beds—only sheets. As usual, he justifies the pigs' actions by threatening Mr. Jones's return. Soon after, the pigs award themselves the additional privilege of waking up an hour late.

By autumn, the windmill is half finished. One night in November, violent winds ravage the farm and destroy the windmill. Napoleon quickly blames the destruction on Snowball. He sentences Snowball to death and offers half a bushel of apples and the title of "Animal Hero, Second Class" to any animal that detains him. There is a track of pig footprints leading to the hedge, which Napoleon attributes to Snowball. Then Napoleon rouses the animals to action, saying, "Forward, comrades! Long live the windmill! Long live Animal Farm!" (83).

Analysis

In Chapter VI, the animals begin working tirelessly to complete the windmill. In this case, we can see the windmill as the first of Stalin's Five Year Plans. The Five Year Plans had the same aim as Lenin's New Economic Policy, which was to stimulate Russian industry and help bring it into the 20th century. Unlike the NEP, which left some control of industry in the people's hands, Stalin's Five Year Plans brought Russian industry under complete government control. Orwell mirrors this pattern in Napoleon's tightening of the reigns on the animal workforce. Napoleon's supposedly "voluntary" but actually compulsory Sunday labor sets him even farther apart from Snowball, who advocated a shorter workweek.

This episode also reflects Stalin's reliance on tactics of deception. Although Stalin was clear with industry leaders about the goals of the Five Year Plans, he continued manipulating the public to foster increased—albeit successful—labor. As in history, the animals of Animal Farm are able to achieve great productivity but do not benefit personally from their efforts. They suffer shortages because for all their work, the windmill (like the heavy industry on which Stalin focused Soviet efforts) cannot yet provide them with energy, much less the basic things they need.

Unlike Napoleon, who opens trade relations with neighboring farms, Stalin was conservative about foreign trade. Rather than representing a specific event in history, Napoleon's decision to conduct business with other farms is another opportunity for Orwell to point out Stalin's hypocrisy and revisionism by means of the pigs' rejection of the original principles of the Rebellion. The very basis for Animalism is the idea that humans are the enemy and not to be trusted—"four legs good, two legs bad." By negotiating with humans, Napoleon undermines Animalism completely at the same time he is reminding the animals that the windmill should be their first priority. By having Napoleon show such disregard for Animalism's tenets, Orwell suggests that Stalin was more a proponent of his personal interests than he was of the cause of Communism. Like Napoleon, Stalin did not seem to believe in the greater good for which he forced his people to work so tirelessly.

Orwell mirrors Stalin's caution in dealing with foreign nations in Napoleon's procurement of an intermediary, Mr. Whymper. Additionally, Whymper represents those countries that traded with the Soviet Union while turning a blind eye to Stalin's abuses. Whymper (whose name suggests whimpering or docility) works purely for profit and never interferes in Animal Farm's affairs.

Orwell also expands his critique of Stalin's revisionist propaganda. The pigs break another of the Seven Commandments when they begin living in the farmhouse and sleeping in beds. Clover and Muriel investigate, only to discover that the commandment has been changed to suit the pigs' desires. Through his smooth talking, Squealer convinces Clover and Muriel that the commandment has always concerned the use of sheets and not beds. In this revision, the allegory serves Orwell particularly well. Stalin and his propagandists plastered the Soviet Union with propaganda in the form of posters, songs, art, and countless other media. Squealer's version of this pattern is to continually re-paint the Seven Commandments to reflect Napoleon's changes in policy. Orwell humorously suggests a Soviet agent going around the Soviet Union, personally scratching out and rewriting the slogans on posters. The point is that the propaganda changes to suit those in power and to keep a controlled acquiescence among the rest.

Chapter VI also continues Orwell's critique of the tactic of intimidation. When Clover and Muriel question the Seven Commandments' accuracy, Squealer threatens them (as usual) with Jones's return. In this chapter, Napoleon's fear tactics culminate with the windmill's destruction. Though natural forces are to blame, Napoleon blames the disaster on Snowball in the same way Stalin considered Trotsky a threat even in exile. In the novel, Napoleon sentences Snowball to death, but we never find out whether his orders are carried out, or if Snowball is even still alive at the time of his sentencing. In history, Stalin eventually did have Trotsky assassinated by a Soviet agent in 1940. Whether Snowball is a true threat to Animal Farm or not, Napoleon makes sure the animals believe Snowball is. In this sense, Snowball represents the nebulous foreign threat of which Stalin kept his people wary. There are now two terrorist enemies to fear, Mr. Jones (even if he has left town, other men remain to be afraid of) and Snowball.

Orwell makes the connection between fear tactics and economic strategy very clear at the end of Chapter VI. Napoleon moves directly from accusing Snowball of destroying the windmill to urging the animals, "Forward, comrades! Long live the windmill! Long live Animal Farm" (83). Napoleon remains a leader the animals are willing to follow—they cannot see another choice, anyway, especially with Mr. Jones and Snowball cast as enemies—but the legitimacy of Napoleon's authority is becoming more and more suspect to the reader.

Summary and Analysis of Chapter VII

The animals work to rebuild the windmill through a bitter, stormy winter, well aware that the human world is watching and hoping for their failure. Because of increasing food shortages, the animals begin to go hungry. Knowing that the humans must not hear of Animal Farm's hardships, Napoleon enlists the sheep to comment about their increasing rations when within earshot of Mr. Whymper. He also has someone lead Mr. Whymper past the food bins, which are filled with sand and topped with grain to look full.

Napoleon appears in public less and less, and when he does, six fierce dogs act as his guards. As there is need for more grain, he has Mr. Whymper arrange a contract to sell four hundred eggs per week. The hens rebel by laying their eggs in the rafters so that the eggs smash on the floor. Napoleon stops the hens' rations and makes feeding a hen punishable by death. Nine hens die, supposedly of coccidiosis, during the five-day strike, after which the hens surrender.

Napoleon negotiates with Mr. Frederick and Mr. Pilkington, who wish to buy Animal Farm's supply of timber. A rumor begins circulating among the animals that Snowball is sneaking into the farm at night and causing mischief. From then on, the animals attribute any misfortune to Snowball's interference. Napoleon arranges a public investigation of Snowball's activities. He surveys the farm and claims to smell Snowball's scent everywhere. The animals are terrified. That evening, Squealer tells the animals that Snowball now belongs to Mr. Frederick, with whom he is plotting to overtake Animal Farm. He claims that Snowball was collaborating with Mr. Jones from the very beginning and claims to have supporting evidence. Squealer also claims that Snowball intended to get the animals killed in the Battle of the Cowshed. When the animals, including Boxer, protest, Squealer invents yet another lie. He claims that Napoleon cried, "Death to Humanity!" during the battle and bit Mr. Jones in the leg. Boxer continues to protest until Squealer tells him that the news is directly from Napoleon. Boxer replies, "If Comrade Napoleon says it, it must be right" (91). Before leaving, Squealer gives Boxer a nasty look and warns the animals that Snowball's secret agents are lurking among them.

Four days later, Napoleon calls an assembly. He wears the medals of "Animal Hero, First Class" and "Animal Hero, Second Class," which he has awarded himself. Napoleon's dogs drag out of the crowd the four pigs that had opposed the cessation of Sunday meetings. The dogs try to drag Boxer out as well, but he deflects them. The pigs confess that they collaborated with Snowball in destroying the windmill and were planning to help Mr. Frederick overtake Animal Farm. They also confess to knowing of Snowball's partnership with Mr. Jones for years. Then the dogs tear out the four pigs' throats. Napoleon asks whether any other animal wishes to confess. Three hens, which had led the hen rebellion, confess that Snowball incited them to revolt in a dream vision. After this, several other animals confess to crimes both great (murder) and small (stealing). Napoleon has them all murdered.

After the public executions, the horrified animals slink away. Boxer blames the evil among them to some "fault" in themselves and suggests that the way to quash it is to work harder. As Clover sits on the knoll with the other animals, she considers how different their current situation is than the ideal Old Major put forth. The animals were supposed to create a society of equality and freedom, not one of "terror and slaughter" (95). Still, Clover thinks Animal Farm is better than it was in the days of Mr. Jones's rule, and her heart remains faithful to it. Unable to put her thoughts into words, Clover leads the animals in singing "Beasts of England."

Suddenly, however, Squealer arrives with a dog escort and forbids the animals from singing the anthem, for Napoleon has abolished it. He explains that the Rebellion has now ended with the slaughter of the unfaithful and that, being a song of the Rebellion, "Beasts of England" has no further purpose. The animals are now to sing Minimus's anthem, which begins with the lyrics: "Animal Farm, Animal Farm, / Never through me shalt thou come to harm!"

Analysis

In Chapter VII, Orwell focuses again on the gap between the tirelessness of the animals' efforts and the benefits they receive. We discussed earlier that, because Stalin focused more on heavy industry than on consumer products, the Soviet people faced shortages of the things they needed the most. Because of chronic shortages in the Soviet Union, there arose the cliché of standing in line for most anything one wanted, including food and toilet paper. When one wanted to purchase a bigger item, such as a car, one was put on the end of a seemingly interminable list. On a side note, Stalin's focus on heavy industry corresponded with his name—meaning steel—which he chose for himself (Stalin was born with the much more ethnically-specific surname Dzhugashivili).

Napoleon begins to shelter himself from public scrutiny and makes Squealer and the dogs do his dirty work. This corresponds with Stalin's habit of being a figure in the shadows. Stalin gave orders from the comfort of his office, while the propagandists and secret police meted out his demands and punishments. The negotiations over the timber represent Stalin's export of the products of heavy industry. Napoleon's waffling between Pilkington and Frederick also mirrors Stalin's caution in dealing with foreign nations.

Meanwhile, in order to distract the animals from their hardships and frustrations, Napoleon increases the amount of propaganda on Animal Farm. Squealer, his agent as usual, cultivates the idea that Snowball is lurking on the perimeter of Animal Farm and plotting mischief against the animals. Napoleon also makes a personal and very public show of claiming to smell Snowball's scent all around the farm. By giving the impression that Snowball is everywhere, Napoleon at ones makes Snowball, a concrete entity, into a nebulous threat and creates an atmosphere of almost palpable fear: "The animals were thoroughly frightened. It seemed to them as though Snowball were some kind of invisible influence, pervading the air about them and menacing them with all kinds of dangers" (89). By personally investigating Snowball's whereabouts, Napoleon keeps himself tied to the greater good in the public's eyes. At once, they feel frightened and also cared for, but they attribute the former feeling to Snowball and the latter to Napoleon.

Soon enough, Napoleon turns Snowball from an outside threat into a pervasive internal threat. Boxer unwittingly gives Squealer the idea when he protests Squealer's revision of Snowball's heroism. Only after Boxer challenges him does Snowball first warn the animals that Snowball's secret agents have infiltrated their ranks. Here, Orwell satirizes Stalin's intensification of fear tactics. In Stalin's Soviet Union, people of every gender, age, and profession were suspected of treachery. Many were forced to confess to things they did not do, all in the name of keeping the public subdued by fear. At this point, we should recall that the Red Terror, the first organized attempt to stamp out anti-Communist sentiment in the Soviet Union, was Lenin's prerogative. Therefore it predated Trotsky and Stalin's debates as well as Trotsky's expulsion. It stands to reason that Orwell skips over the Red Terror in order to assign all terrorist tactics to Napoleon (as opposed to including Snowball). Orwell's experiences in the Spanish Civil War, in which he fought on the side of Trotskyists, may have informed this omission as well.

In any case, Napoleon's execution assembly represents the Moscow Trials and the Great Purge, Stalin's widespread campaign to suppress any and all dissent in the Soviet Union. Indeed, this was a far cry from the cooperation and good cheer with which the Animalism revolution began. In the Soviet Union, it began as a "cleansing" of the Communist Party and was expanded to one of the entire, vast Soviet population, among which tens of millions were killed or deported. In the Moscow Trials of 1936-1938, Stalin incriminated many party leaders, charging them with crimes ranging from conspiracy to attempted assassination. The accused gave their confessions, seemingly freely in front of a general assembly, just as Napoleon's accused give theirs in front of all the other animals. This gave lookers-on a reason to believe that the traitors were rightfully accused, another belief we see repeated in Animal Farm. As Orwell suggests in the text, Stalin (and Napoleon) staged the confessions by using violence and fear tactics to coerce the accused. Witnesses at the trials also gave scripted testimony in order to force guilt upon the accused. Stalin had the accused traitors executed (or, if they were lucky, expelled) just as Napoleon has the dogs rip out the throats of the supposed traitors. Despite the publicity of the Moscow Trials, Stalin often had torture and executions performed in secrecy. Orwell makes Napoleon's purge not only public but especially cruel in order to shed light on the magnitude and barbarism of Stalin's purges. It is one thing to hear of an execution by humans against humans for political reasons, quite another to contemplate the image of fierce dogs tearing out traitors' throats.

The Soviet population became terrified of execution and internment in forced labor camps called Gulags. In the novel, the animals' immediate response to the purge is fear and disillusionment. Shaken, Clover and the other animals try to take comfort in "Beasts of England"—they know that something has gone terribly, terribly wrong but cannot quite describe what or how. They want to focus on the positive ideas of freedom and abundance. Squealer shatters even that comfort when he announces that the song is obsolete and therefore forbidden. We can assume that the real reason Napoleon abolishes it is that, since the animals have committed it to memory, he cannot revise it like the Seven Commandments. Therefore, he forces the animals to forget it, along with the tenets of their beloved Animalism, to be replaced with a new song and new values that are looking more and more like the values under which Mr. Jones ran the farm.

Summary and Analysis of Chapter VIII

Once the terror abates, some of the animals recall the Sixth Commandment, "No animal shall kill any other animal." Clover again asks Muriel to read to her from the wall, only to find that the Sixth Commandment has been changed to: "No animal shall kill any other animal without cause" (98). Clover and Muriel convince themselves that the commandment has always been that way and decide that treachery justifies murder after all. The animals work even harder than in the previous year. On Sundays Squealer assures them, by reading statistics from a sheet of paper, that their efforts are increasing production many times over. The animals can do nothing but believe Squealer. They can scarcely remember life before the Rebellion.

Napoleon restricts his public appearances further to about once a month. He is said to eat separately from the other pigs, using the fine china. He also decrees that the gun be fired every year on his birthday. The animals now call Napoleon "our Leader, Comrade Napoleon." Just as the animals attribute all misfortunes to Snowball, they now attribute all success and luck to Napoleon. Minimus composes a poem called "Comrade Napoleon," which Napoleon has inscribed on the wall across from the Seven Commandments, where Squealer also paints his portrait.

Napoleon continues to negotiate with Mr. Frederick and Mr. Pilkington, though the timber remains unsold. Rumors of Mr. Frederick's plans to overthrow the farm continue. In the summer, three hens confess to plotting against Napoleon's life and are executed instantly. After that, Napoleon increases his security even more and enlists a pig named Pinkeye to be his taster, lest someone attempt to poison him. Napoleon finally agrees to sell the timber to Pilkington, as well as to engage in regular trade with Foxwood. Meanwhile, rumors about Frederick's coming invasion, as well as his cruel practices at Pinchfield, begin to circulate. One day, Napoleon announces that he never planned to do business with Frederick at all. He makes the messenger pigeons change their slogan from "Death to Humanity" to "Death to Frederick" (103). He also, strangely, forbids them from going to Foxwood.

The wheat fields turn out to be filled with weeds, a misfortune that the animals blame promptly on Snowball. A gander confesses to knowing about the plot to mix weed seeds with the wheat seeds and commits suicide. To bring further ignominy upon Snowball's memory, Squealer disseminates a rumor that Snowball never received the title of "Animal Hero, First Class" at all. As usual, he is able to quell any questions that arise from his rewriting of history.

At last the windmill is finished, with walls twice as thick as before. The animals are very proud of their achievement. Napoleon names the windmill "Napoleon Mill." Two days later, Napoleon calls a meeting to announce that he has sold the timber to Frederick, not Pilkington. He denounces Foxwood and makes the pigeons change their slogan to "Death to Pilkington." Napoleon claims that Frederick had never planned to invade Animal Farm and that he was not as cruel as rumored. Moreover, Snowball has never been at Foxwood or been Frederick's collaborator; in reality, he has been Pilkington's longtime collaborator. The pigs are proud of Napoleon's shrewdness. They believe Napoleon's claim that his relationship with Pilkington was just a pretense to get Frederick to raise his bid. Even cleverer, Napoleon refused to let Frederick pay for the timber with a check, instead demanding cash that he will use to buy the windmill machinery. Napoleon goes so far as to hold a special meeting where the animals can inspect the banknotes.

Three days later, Whymper informs Napoleon that the banknotes are forgeries. Napoleon sentences Frederick to death by boiling alive and tries to reconcile with Pilkington. The next morning, Frederick and his armed men overtake the farm. Napoleon considers calling Pilkington for help, but Pilkington sends a note that says, "Serves you right." As the animals watch helplessly, Frederick and his men blow up the windmill. After that, the animals put up a fight and manage to chase the men off. Squealer, who was not in the battle, has the gun fired as a sign of victory. For the first time, Boxer's faith in the value of hard work begins to flag. However, Napoleon devotes two days to celebrating the victory at the newly named Battle of the Windmill and burying the slain. He also gives himself the title, "Order of the Green Banner."

A few days later, the pigs discover a store of whisky, which they begin consuming. The morning after, the pigs do not show up for work. Squealer finally emerges to inform the animals that Napoleon is dying, a fact that the animals blame on Snowball. He announces Napoleon's final declaration: drinking alcohol should be punishable by death. However, Napoleon recovers and, soon after, asks Whymper to procure information on how to brew alcohol. He also designates a field for the propagation of barley. Soon after, a strange episode occurs. One midnight, a crash in the barn awakens the animals. They rush there only to discover Squealer with a broken ladder and a can of paint. Benjamin seems to understand what is happening but declines to share his insight with the others. However, a few days later, Muriel notices that the Fifth Commandment has been changed from "No animal shall drink alcohol" to "No animal shall drink alcohol to excess" (113).

Analysis

Napoleon's revisionism continues with the alterations of the commandments. Worst of all is the reversal from "No animal shall kill any other animal" to "No animal shall kill any other animal *without cause*." This particular revision may strike a particularly deep chord with readers on the parallel between the original Commandment and the Biblical commandment "Thou shalt not kill." On that note, we should notice that by this point, Moses is absent from Animal Farm along with the morality he represents and his vision of Sugarcandy Mountain, which could help the animals through their terror. Napoleon adds to his array of propaganda the reading of optimistic statistics. Stalin's Five Year Plans were successful, especially considering how much catching up Russia had to do, but they did not meet up to his exceptionally high projections. Maintaining appearances was deemed vital to the regime's international reputation.

At this point, Napoleon can trust that his terrorist tactics have made the animals submissive. They cannot believe in their own safety, so they embrace any good news they can get, and good news arrives to them almost exclusively in the form of propaganda. They have lost the ability to judge their success or their quality of life because they cannot remember what life was like before or just after the Rebellion. The animals have also become immune to the type of outrage that their leaders' deceit might arouse in someone with a democratic education and mindset. Even when they catch Squealer in the act of revising the Seven Commandments, they are too subdued to protest. The animals have taken on Benjamin's quality of apathy, not because they are naturally apathetic like him, but because Napoleon has molded and terrorized them to be that way. In the same way, the Soviet populace adjusted to Stalin's tactics of fear and manipulation. Powerless to change anything, they grew to accept it. In psychology this might be called a denial, a defense mechanism, or a coping mechanism. Again, the nobles, who tended to have better educations than the working class, had fled.

As the animals are forced to live an increasingly restricted lifestyle, Napoleon and the pigs are continually awarding themselves privileges and taking an unfair share of the rations. Historically, this corresponds to Stalin's privileging of the Communist elite. While the typical Soviet citizen worked hard and gained little, the typical member of the Communist elite had access to everything from fancy consumer goods to summer houses in the country. During the 1930s, it became increasingly difficult for people to join the ranks of the Communist elite. Orwell reflects this in Animal Farm, where there is absolutely no social mobility. Pigs alone have access to privileges such as sleeping in beds and drinking alcohol. We should recall that the seeds of this extreme class stratification, contrary to the tenets of Animalism and to Marxism-Leninism, began very early on when the pigs appropriated the milk supply. Orwell introduces the pigs' privileges early and increases them gradually to show how insidious and therefore successful Stalin's policies could be. People can be subjugated severely when the subjugation is enacted by degrees.

The events of Chapter VIII cover the historical events of: Hiter's ascension to power in Germany, the Nazi-Soviet non-aggression pact, and Germany's invasion of the Soviet Union. Napoleon continues to be suspicious of Frederick just as Stalin kept one eye open as Hitler ascended to power in Germany. The stories of animal torture on Frederick's farm are meant to symbolize the reports of atrocities coming out of Nazi Germany. The rumors are not substantiated in Animal Farm, presumably because the truth about the scale and severity of Hitler's atrocities did not emerge fully until after World War II. Napoleon's tightening leash on Animal Farm's consciousness is reflected in his interactions with the messenger pigeons. The pigeons, which were formerly his mouthpieces, are now forbidden from flying over the neighboring farms. Presumably, Napoleon does not want them to undermine his ever-changing opinions about Frederick and Pilkington.

In 1939, the Soviet Union and Nazi Germany signed a non-aggression pact that promised neutrality and cooperation between the two nations. In Animal Farm, Napoleon's trade agreement with Frederick symbolizes this pact. Napoleon does not trust Frederick completely, as shown in his unwillingness to accept a check. In the same way Stalin was wary of Hitler and his goals, perhaps seeing some of his own ruthlessness and ambition in Hitler's eyes. Napoleon's distrust of Frederick soon turns out to be true, just as Stalin was right not to trust Hitler completely. Hitler's forces invaded the Soviet Union in 1941, an event that Orwell mirrors in Frederick's attack on Animal Farm. He summarizes the incredible damage that the Nazis did before their defeat in the destruction of the windmill.

Pilkington's neutrality during the conflict and his not-so-neutral message, "Serves you right," satirize the Allies' initial hesitance to respond during World War II. World War II devastated the Soviet population, which lost over twenty million people. Orwell reflects the magnitude of the Soviet Union's loss in Boxer's flagging enthusiasm. Even he, the bastion of positive thinking, finds it difficult to recoup after the Battle of the Windmill. With Animal Farm so isolationist and duplicitous toward the human world (compare modern-day North Korea), it is no wonder that it faces withering shortages, demoralization, and tyranny within and hostility everywhere without.

Summary and Analysis of Chapter IX

Boxer's split hoof, an injury from the battle, taxes him; still he will not let it deter him from rebuilding the windmill before he reaches retirement age. When they first formed Animal Farm, the animals had agreed on fixed retirement ages and pensions. The winter is bitter again. Rations, save the pigs' and dogs', are reduced--"readjusted," as Squealer says. To appease the animals, Squealer reads the animals more statistics to make them believe that their lives are better than in the days of Mr. Jones's rule. The animals are overworked, underfed, and cold, but they are happy to believe Squealer.

Thirty-one young pigs now live on the farm, all of them parented by Napoleon. He makes plans to build them a schoolhouse and discourages them from interacting with other types of animals. He also instates two rules of pig superiority: other animals must stand aside on the path to let pigs pass, and pigs are allowed to wear green ribbons on their tails on Sundays. Napoleon also awards himself the privilege of eating sugar. Still, times are hard on the farm, and the animals struggle to make ends meet. The chickens are forced to lay six hundred eggs per week to sell in town and can barely keep any for hatching. Rations are reduced again, and the animals are not allowed lanterns in their stalls anymore in order to save oil. Meanwhile, the pigs seem to be flourishing.

Towards the end of winter, the animals smell a new scent in the wind, which they discover is from the barley Napoleon has begun to cook. Soon after, the pigs announce that all barley is reserved for them. Each pig gets a pint of beer added to his rations, with Napoleon getting half a gallon. To distract the animals from their hardship, Napoleon increases the amount of propaganda on the farm. This includes songs, speeches, poems, statistics, marches, and his newly created Spontaneous Demonstrations, in which the animals celebrate their victories. The animals enjoy the Spontaneous Demonstrations, which remind them of their freedom and self-sufficiency.

In April, Napoleon declares Animal Farm a Republic, and the animals elect Napoleon unanimously as president. His new propaganda claims Snowball was not a covert human collaborator, but an open one who charged into battle on the human side yelling, "Long Live Humanity!" (119). In mid-summer, Moses returns from a long absence. His stories of Sugarcandy Mountain return with him. The other animals enjoy the stories, with the exception of the pigs. Boxer and the other animals work feverishly to complete their tasks, which now include building the schoolhouse for the young pigs. One day, Boxer overworks himself so much that he collapses, unable to get up. In his sickly state, he expresses a wish to retire early along with Benjamin. The animals fetch Squealer, who relays Napoleon's decision to send Boxer to the veterinary hospital in Willingdon.

Over the next two days, Boxer lies in his stall and takes doses from "a large bottle of pink medicine" that the pigs send from the farmhouse. He expresses his wish to spend his final years learning the rest of the alphabet. One afternoon, a van comes to take Boxer away. It has "lettering on its side and a sly-looking man in a low-crowned bowler hat sitting on the driver's seat." The hopeful animals wish Boxer goodbye, but Benjamin breaks their revelry by reading the lettering on the side of the van: "Alfred Simmons, Horse Slaughterer and Glue Boiler, Willingdon. Dealer in Hides and Bone-Meal. Kennels Supplied" (123). The animals panic and try to get Boxer to escape. He tries to get out of the van, but he has grown too weak to break the door. The animals try to appeal to the horses drawing the van, but they do not understand the situation.

Boxer never returns, but three days later the pigs announce that he died in the hospital despite receiving the best care. Squealer claims to have been present at Boxer's death, a tale he relates emotionally to the other animals. He claims that Boxer's last words were, "Forward, Comrades! ... Forward in the name of the Rebellion" and "Long live Animal Farm! Long live Comrade Napoleon! Napoleon is always right" (125). Squealer also claims that the van belongs to the veterinarian, who had recently bought it from the horse slaughterer and had not yet managed to paint over the lettering. These stories satisfy the animals. The next Sunday, Napoleon promises to honor Boxer with a special wreath and a memorial banquet. On the day the banquet is to be held, a large crate arrives at Animal Farm. That night, the pigs are rowdy inside the farmhouse and do not wake up until noon the next day. The animals hear a rumor that the pigs had bought a case of whisky.

Analysis

World War II devastated not only the Soviet Union's populace but also its economy. Agriculture and factory production, which the people had worked so tirelessly to fortify in previous decades, were left in shambles. In Animal Farm, the windmill represents the Soviet people's economic progress. Frederick and his men ruin the windmill in one fell swoop just as the Nazis destroyed the Soviet Union's hard-earned progress. In the Five Year Plans after World War II, Stalin had no choice but to focus on recouping the Soviet Union's losses. In the same vein, Napoleon rededicates the animals to the windmill's construction. Boxer's attitude after the war represents the toll that the war took on the Soviet people's morale. Still, they managed to rally just as Boxer does, despite even harsher shortages than ever.

Despite harsh conditions for the rest of the animals, the pigs are flourishing. Napoleon has managed to parent thirty-one new pigs, which he plans to make disciples of his theories by building a schoolhouse. (This may be a reference to the Thirty Tyrants of ancient Greece, only a little worse.) As usual, Napoleon makes the animals complicit in their own oppression, this time by forcing them to build the schoolhouse on top of their reconstructive and regular workload. Napoleon's abuses become even more blatant and more reminiscent of Jones's behavior when he awards pigs the right of way on the path. The other animals must stand aside in deference to the pigs, which is the sort of behavior a peasant under the feudal system would have to display in his master's presence. The pigs even assume Mollie's two favorite habits: eating sugar and wearing ribbons in their tails. If we recall that Mollie represents the imperial elite, we can see how far Animal Farm has regressed.

By making Napoleon's abuses so blatant, Orwell exposes the fact that stratification is inevitable in the hands of corrupt leaders and that power and greed are cyclical. The pigs begin the book by carrying out Old Major's ideals of a working-class rebellion just as the Bolsheviks overthrew the czar with Marxism-Leninism in mind. Then, just as Stalin and the Soviet elite came to resemble the imperialists they so despised, Napoleon and the pigs take on human characteristics. This—emulating humans—is the very thing against which Major warned the animals in his meeting. Readers are progressively horrified by the new outrages and betrayals committed by the pigs.

Orwell focuses on propaganda again in Chapter IX. This time he focuses less on the manipulative nature of propaganda and more on its grandeur. Napoleon's Spontaneous Demonstrations are especially pompous and gay, with a cockerel marching in front of the procession. The Spontaneous Demonstrations also involve the animals directly in the propaganda machine. More than singing songs or chanting maxims, they are now marching around the farm to celebrate Animal Farm's glory. The gun, originally intended to solemnly mark the anniversaries of battles, is now used liberally to stir the animals' loyalties. (See the Related Links for a clip from a Soviet propaganda film, keeping the Spontaneous Demonstrations in mind.) Further proving their submission, the animals find the increase in propaganda uplifting: "But if there were hardships to be borne, they were partly offset by the fact that life nowadays had a greater dignity than it had had before. There were more songs, more speeches, more processions ... They found it comforting to be reminded that all the work they did was for their own benefit. ... They were able to forget that their bellies were empty, at least part of the time" (117-118). Orwell comes close to sympathy for the animals in this passage, where he seems to suggest that in addition to the animals' gullibility, they have a desperate need to be uplifted, even by means as false and ridiculous as the Spontaneous Demonstrations. Moses' return also supplies them with much-needed inspiration, although the pigs are wary of his competing influence.

Orwell breaks such reverie with the story of Boxer's illness and murder. By this point, Orwell has repeated the pigs' abuses so many times that the reader may be as desperate as the animals for some relief. But Orwell wastes no time in reminding us that propaganda is just the totalitarian government's machine of deception. Napoleon feels no affinity for Boxer, despite that animal's years of tireless work on Animal Farm's behalf. This is because Napoleon feels entitled to the animals' hard work just as Stalin was more concerned with his own goals than with his people's well being. Napoleon sends Boxer off to the slaughter for profit without seeming to have any second thoughts except for finding a way to explain the betrayal to the other animals. Adding insult to injury, he uses Boxer's murder as an opportunity for more propaganda, having Squealer relate to the animals Boxer's supposed patriotic last words. Then he and the pigs celebrate their latest feat of deception and violence by drinking the case of whisky. While the pigs are becoming more like humans, they are becoming the kind of humans whom others would call animals for their cruelty and irrationality.

Summary and Analysis of Chapter X

After a few years, the only animals that even remember the Rebellion are Clover, Benjamin, Moses, and some of the pigs. Muriel, Bluebell, Jessie, and Pincher have died. Mr. Jones has died in a home for alcoholics. Still, no animal has retired, and no pasture has been put aside for retired animals. Napoleon and Squealer have both become very fat. The farm is bigger, thanks to land purchased from Mr. Pilkington, and now features a threshing machine and hay elevator. The windmill is finished, but the animals use it to mill corn for a profit instead of to generate electricity as planned. Napoleon puts the animals to work building an additional windmill, which he promises will supply electricity. However, he discourages the animals from dreaming of luxury, saying, "The truest happiness … [lies] in working hard and living frugally" (129).

The pigs and dogs continue to do no manual labor, instead devoting themselves to organizational work that the other animals are "too ignorant to understand" (130). This includes writing up notes and burning them promptly after. Propaganda and pride in living on the only animal-owned farm in England continue to distract the animals from their hardships. One day, Squealer takes all the sheep out to an overgrown patch of land on the far side of the farm. Over the next week, he claims to be teaching them a song, and no one sees them. On the day the sheep return, Clover alerts the other animals to a disturbing fact: Squealer and the other pigs are walking two-footed, on their hind legs. The sheep break into a chorus of, "Four legs good, two legs better!" Benjamin accompanies Clover to the barn wall, where he deigns to read to her for the first time. In place of the Seven Commandments there is now a single maxim: "All animals are equal / But some animals are more equal than others" (133).

The animals discover that the pigs are buying a telephone and have subscribed to several magazines. Napoleon takes to smoking Mr. Jones's pipe, and the other pigs take to wearing Mrs. Jones's clothes. Napoleon begins wearing Mr. Jones's dress clothes and awards "his favorite sow" the privilege of wearing Mrs. Jones's Sunday dress. One day, Napoleon invites human visitors to tour the farm. That night, the animals spy into the farmhouse and see the pigs dining with the humans. According to Mr. Pilkington's toast, they are celebrating the end of their bad relations. Touring Animal Farm has impressed him and the other farmers to follow Animal Farm's example and give their animals more work and less food. Napoleon says he wants to cooperate with the other farms and confirms that he and the pigs co-own the farm's title-deeds. He states that the animals will no longer be calling each other "Comrade" or marching past Old Major's skull (a practice he denies understanding anyway). In addition, the flag has been changed to a plain green without the symbols of the Rebellion. Even further, Animal Farm shall again be referred to as "The Manor Farm." The pigs and humans begin to play poker, and a fight erupts when Napoleon and Pilkington both put down the Ace of Spades at the same time. As the animals witness the pigs and humans quarreling over their poker game, they cannot distinguish between them.

Analysis

Orwell fast-forwards to a time when Animal Farm has undergone a great deal of turnover. Only a few animals that remember the Rebellion remain, and their memories of it are faint. Napoleon has rewritten the animals' history to the extent that they feel they no longer have one. He has also manipulated language to the extent that it is meaningless. We see this reflected in the maxim, "All animals are equal / But some animals are more equal than others." The concept of "more equal" is mathematically impossible, but the animals are too disillusioned and brainwashed to notice. In all the years since the Rebellion, not a single animal has gotten the rewards that he was promised or that was experienced so briefly in the days immediately following the Rebellion. In history, Chapter X corresponds to a time somewhere in the distant future, beyond the realm of Orwell's own experience. It is, therefore, the manifestation of his pessimistic conjectures about the future of totalitarianism. In this chapter, Orwell slowly and firmly crushes our hopes along with the animals'. In the end, the pigs have all the tangible fruits of Animal Farm's labor while the animals are left with only empty promises. The windmill, the cause for which countless animals labored and died, has been diverted from its original purpose of supplying electricity. Not even Clover and Benjamin, who are by this time very old, have been allowed to retire. While wearing clothing, smoking pipes, and eating sugar, Napoleon still has the nerve to tell the animals, "The truest happiness … [lies] in working hard and living frugally" (129). It is a harrowing, dystopic future.

In the pessimistic vein for which he became known, Orwell imagines a future in which not only the Soviet Union, but also the Allies, become totalitarian. We see this reflected in Pilkington's speech at the banquet. He not only agrees to collaborate with Napoleon, but vows to emulate Napoleon's harsh standards of labor and living on his own farm. In his own toast, Napoleon seals the door on Animal Farm's history and breaks the last ties with its original tenets. He changes the farm's name back to "Manor Farm," as though the trials, triumphs, and abuses of the past many years never happened. It is clear that he intends to erase the memory of Animal Farm from history. Stalin and Hitler were both known to do this in educating the youth in their countries. Most likely, the textbooks in Napoleon's schoolhouse will severely skew the truth about Animal Farm, if they mention the name "Animal Farm" at all. Napoleon breaks the final tie with Major when he denies knowing why the animals march past his skull in ceremonious fashion. He is erasing knowledge not just of the ideas that Major stood for, but also all the things he himself authored.

The poker game is multiply symbolic. First, it represents the carelessness with which totalitarian leaders treat their people. The animals are like cards in the gambler's hands, subject to whim and chance. When Napoleon and Pilkington fight over the Ace of Spades (which proves that at least one of them had a card up his sleeve), they foreshadow the international disagreements and struggles that are sure to follow the temporary postwar peace. In this symbolic meaning, Orwell foreshadows the Cold War even though it did not begin in earnest until after the book was published. Pigs and humans are equals at the table, more or less, and rivals once the game is over.

Orwell demonstrates the fact that oppression is cyclical and the oppressed becomes the oppressor when given the chance. By the novel's end, the pigs are indistinguishable from the humans not only in behavior but also in appearance. Their transformation is complete when they adopt two-legged walking. They treat the animals in the autocratic manner of Jones. In this sense, the story has come full circle.

The future Orwell creates for Animal Farm does not correspond neatly with Imperial Russia. Before the Rebellion, the animals lived under Jones's total control but had the advantage, the bliss, of ignorance. Now they are living under Napoleon's total control, having been enlightened to the possibility of freedom and, it seems, still under the impression that they are free but no longer understanding what true freedom would be. This is consistent with Orwell's belief that 20th-century autocrats such as Hitler and Stalin were of a new and more dangerous kind than the dictators of the past.

Animal Farm is a warning about autocrats who take over socialist ideals for their own aggrandizement. Is there any chance for socialism if human nature is such that the lust for greed and power brings forth leaders who take control and betray its ideals, over against passive and uneducated populations? The capitalist, democratic alternative is to channel that lust into productive work and to limit the power of government to control the freedoms of the people. This alternative creates or aggravates inequalities—one might say that there will always be pigs, dogs, horses, cats, and the rest—but is far preferable to totalitarian control. The challenge for Orwell or for anyone who promotes socialist ideals is to find a practical way to circumvent the abuses that the pigs of Animal Farm so easily commit. But since the novel is a reflection of the challenges of the 1940s rather than a political treatise, Orwell has done quite enough in demonstrating, clearly and horrifyingly, the nature and scope of the challenges to be faced.

Suggested Essay Questions

1. How is *Animal Farm* a satire of Stalinism or generally of totalitarianism?

   Answer: A good way to answer this question is to pick a specific example of totalitarianism in any country, historical or current, and explain how the ideas Orwell puts forth in *Animal Farm* apply to it. Go back and forth between the historical facts and the events of the novel. Note the actions of the leaders, the mechanisms of fear and power, and the reactions of the people over time.
2. Elucidate the symbolism inherent in the characters' names.

   Answer: The symbolism ranges from the obvious to the more cryptic. Compare Napoleon with the historical Frenchman and Moses with the figure from the Bible. Take Snowball as representative of something that grows larger and more forceful. Squealer has something to do with the spoken word. Boxer suggests strength. Make sure to consider each character at various stages of the story and to use specific examples from the text.
3. What does the narrator do, or fail to do, that makes the story's message possible?

   Answer: The narrator lets the story tell itself to a large degree by relating what is said and done without moralization and reflection. The narrator speaks from the perspective of the animals other than the pigs, a kind of observer who can point out the significant details without interfering. The reader then can draw his own conclusions about the symbolism, concordance with historical events, and the awfulness of the events themselves.
4. What does the windmill represent?

   Answer: The windmill's symbolic meaning changes during the course of the novel and means different things to different characters. It is to be for electricity but ends up being for economic production. As it is built, it is a locus of work without benefit and a medium of the pigs' power. For the humans, it is a dangerous symbol of the growing power of the farm. Consider also the relationship between the windmill and the biblical Tower of Babel.
5. What role does the written word play in *Animal Farm*?

   Answer: Literacy is a source of power and a vehicle for propaganda. Some examples to consider are the Seven Commandments, "Beasts of England," the child's book, the manuals, the magazines, and the horse-slaughterer's van.
6. Examine the Seven Commandments and the way they change during the course of the novel from Old Major's death to the banquet Napoleon holds

with the farmers.

Answer: The commandments begin as democratic ideals of equality and fraternity in a common animal identity, but they end in inequality when some animals are "more equal" than others. As the pigs take more control and assume their own liberties, they unilaterally change the commandments to fit their own desires. Consider especially the interactions between Clover, Muriel, and Squealer surrounding the Seven Commandments, determining how easy it is to change the fundamental rules of society on the farm, where most of the animals can do no better than to remember that four legs are good and two legs are bad.

7. Would *Animal Farm* be more effective as a nonfiction political treatise about the same subject?

   Answer: Given the success of the novel, it is hard to see why Orwell might have chosen a different genre for his message. A nonfiction account would have had to work more accurately with the history, while Orwell's fiction has the benefit of ordering and shaping events in order to make the points as clear as possible from a theoretical and symbolic point of view. A political treatise could be more effective in treating the details and theoretical understandings at greater length and with more nuances, but the readership and audience for such a work would therefore become quite different as well, so the general population would be less likely to hear Orwell's warnings.

8. Can we perceive much of Orwell himself in the novel?

   Answer: Orwell seems to be most like the narrator, who tells the story from the perspective of experience with the events related. We know from Orwell's history that he was a champion of the working class and did not much like the idea of being in a role where he had to exercise power to control people under him. Orwell seems to be a realist about the prospects for the socialist ideals he otherwise would promote.

9. Compare *Animal Farm* with Orwell's other famous novel, *1984*.

   Answer: Consider the ways in which both novels are allegories with a political message against the evils of state control and totalitarianism. How does totalitarian control affect the illiterate versus those who are educated and wish to exercise their human rights? Compare the political regimes in the two novels. Does the relative anonymity of the leaders affect the reactions of the people?

10. Pick a classic fairy tale or fable and examine it in comparison with *Animal Farm*.

    Answer: A good way to answer such a question is to consider the function of animals as characters. For instance, each of the Three Little Pigs expresses a different approach to planning for the future and managing risk, which can lead to an analysis of how each character represents a moral or physical quality. In terms of narration, note the degree to which the narrator lets the characters speak in their own voices and lets the plot play out without editorializing. In terms of structure, consider how critical events shatter the calm (such as getting lost in the woods or encountering an enemy) and lead to a moral once some kind of order (for better or for worse) is restored.

A Brief History of the Soviet Union, 1917-1944

Before the revolution of 1917, Russia had been an imperial autocracy since the reign of Peter the Great in the 1700s. Russia had become a great world power after the defeat of Napoleon's army in the 1800s. During the 1800s, the desire for social and political change in Russia began to grow, with revolts and the formation of political organizations. In the early 1900s, Russia had splintered politically into two factions: the Bolsheviks, lead by Vladimir Lenin, and the Mensheviks. By 1917, Russia found itself in the midst of World War I, demoralized and facing shortages and other hardships.

In the February Revolution of 1917, Czar Nicholas II abdicated his position as leader of Russia, ending the nation's imperial rule under the Romanov Dynasty. For more than half a year after the czar's abdication, an ineffective provisional government ran the vast empire. During that time, Lenin returned from exile and regrouped his strength and support. Lenin saw in the army's dissatisfaction with the provisional government an opportunity to gain control. He guided the soviets, his fellow communists, in establishing good relations with Russia's troops. Helping Lenin were Leon Trotsky, another former exile, and Joseph Stalin. On October 24, 1917, Lenin and his collaborators launched a successful, full-scale coup against the provisional government, which came to be known as the October Revolution. They established a new government based on the tenets of communism, which included the equal distribution of wealth and the promotion of atheism and gender equality.

Lenin's rise to power did not ensure further success or popular satisfaction immediately, although his New Economic Policy (NEP) increased agricultural production. Russia met with the Central Powers at the Treaty of Brest-Litovsk in 1918, losing a significant portion of its territory to other nations. Meanwhile, Russia's former elite as well as its working and farming class were becoming dissatisfied with the new government and were garnering foreign support for their cause. In response to the public's dissent, the leaders formed the Red Army, led by Trotsky. The Red Army launched an internal campaign of terror called the Red Terror, in which it intended to root out and kill the "internal enemy" of anti-Communism. Thousands of people, many of whom were only suspected of being anti-Communist, were slaughtered in unthinkably cruel ways. That conflict turned into the Russian Civil War, which lasted until 1921 and terrorized Russia's citizenry. Lenin saw the Civil War through, including the creation of the Soviet Union in 1922, but died in 1924. (His embalmed body is still preserved in a mausoleum in Red Square, and it is a popular tourist attraction.) In his wake Lenin left Trotsky and Stalin, both power-hungry politicians, to battle for Russia's leadership.

In Lenin's absence, Trotsky's oratorical acumen proved no match for Stalin, who defeated him easily with the help of important internal alliances. Stalin expatriated him, along with many other leaders, in the Great Purge and eventually had Trotsky assassinated in exile. For the next quarter of a century, Stalin was the leader of the Soviet Union. Determined to bring Russia out of its long-standing economic deficiency, including the Grain Crisis, and recoup the losses sustained in World War I, he abandoned NEP and launched several "Five Year Plans," aggressive campaigns to increase the country's productivity while bringing the economy completely under government control. The plans were successful but resulted in dissatisfaction among the citizens of the Soviet Union. In order to prevent them from rebelling, Stalin used the tactics of deception and terror. He began a series of "purges" in which he executed anyone suspected of harboring sentiments contrary to his ideas. Determined to protect himself and his government from treachery, Stalin not only increased the government's internal espionage, carried out by the NKVD and its subsidiary, the KGB, but he turned Soviet citizens against one another. Terrified of imprisonment, torture, work in the Gulags (labor camps) and execution, people spied on and turned in their coworkers, neighbors, and even family members. In total, tens of millions of people experienced Stalin's terror firsthand, and those who did not knew someone who had.

With the Soviet Union's internal affairs under tight (and violent) control, Stalin focused his attention on international affairs. He and his government took Hitler's ascension very seriously, especially considering the losses Russia suffered in World War I. For this reason, in the 1930s Stalin lent Soviet support to Spain in the Spanish Civil War, in which the country was trying to defend itself against the German and Japanese forces of fascism. (This is the war in which George Orwell fought, against fascism but also against the Soviets.) Despite Stalin's mistrust of Adolf Hitler, the Soviet Union signed a non-aggression pact with Germany in 1939 and continued to trade with Hitler's nation. When World War II broke out in September 1939 and in 1941, Germany broke the non-aggression pact and invaded the Soviet Union. World War II took a terrible toll on the Western parts of the Soviet Union. This included the nine-hundred-day Siege of Leningrad, in which 1.5 million of the city's citizens died of cold, starvation, or bombardment by the Germans. Despite harsh battles and the loss of more than twenty million citizens, the Soviet Union managed to drive the Nazis out and continued marching westward, seizing control of Berlin in May 1945. A few months later, Animal Farm hit the bookshelves in England and recounted, allegorically, much of this history. Stalin remained in control of the Soviet Union until his death in 1953.

Author of ClassicNote and Sources

Tania Asnes, author of ClassicNote. Completed on May 06, 2008, copyright held by GradeSaver.

Updated and revised Adam Kissel May 31, 2008. Copyright held by GradeSaver.

Davidson, Peter Hobley. George Orwell: A Literary Life. New York: St. Martin's Press, 1996.

O'Neill, Terry, ed. Readings on Animal Farm. San Diego: Greenhaven Press, 1998.

Orwell, George. Animal Farm: A Fairy Story. Orlando: Signet Classics, 1996.

Service, Robert. A History of Modern Russia. Cambridge, Mass.: Harvard University Press, 2005.

Wieczynski, Joseph L., ed. The Modern Encyclopedia of Russian and Soviet History. Gulf Breeze, Fla.: Academic International Press, 1976.

"Dictionary.com." 2008-05-04. <http://www.dictionary.com>.

Menand, Louis. "Honest, Decent, Wrong: The Invention of George Orwell." The New Yorker. 2003-01-27. 2008-05-01. <http://www.newyorker.com/archive/2003/01/27/030127crat_atlarge>.

Orwell, George. "Politics and the English Language." Mount Holyoke College International Relations Program. 1946-04-01. 2008-05-01. <http://www.mtholyoke.edu/acad/intrel/orwell46.htm>.

Orwell, George. "Such, Such Were the Joys." Feedbooks.com. 2008-05-05. <http://www.feedbooks.com/discover/book/1333>.

Essay: Bit and Spur Shall Rust Forever: Hollow Symbols in George Orwell's Animal Farm

by Mike Yank
July 01, 2002

George Orwell's political fable Animal Farm portrays a reenactment of the Russian Revolution, with major characters cast as farm animals and communism renamed "Animalism." True to the historical story, the aristocratic players manipulate the proletariat, deluding them with illusions of dignity and improved living conditions, while masterfully holding all of the power for themselves. Once Napoleon seizes control, he carefully dismantles the Animalistic system Old Major had preached by slowly altering the common symbols of freedom and patriotic sayings, and establishes a devious government at least as unjust as its precursor in its place. The meat of Animalism decays as Marxism did, resulting in a system of desired shape lacking desired thought, grossly symbolized in the following passage by Old Major's remains:

> The skull of old Major, now clean of flesh, had been disinterred from the orchard and set up on a stump at the foot of the flagstaff, behind the gun. After the hoisting of the flag, the animals were required to file past the skull in a reverent manner before entering the barn. -(Animal Farm, 46-47)

Orwell uses symbols in terms of hollowness throughout Animal Farm to portray the empty promises behind false front the pigs put up, and in turn the tragedy of the animals celebrating their own demise. In addition to the skull, Orwell also "hollows out" the meanings of the Manor Farm flag and the farm anthem to show the sad fall of the utopian farm.

Once Napoleon chases away Snowball and reconstructs Animal Farm, he imposes many new procedures, among them the revamping of Sunday meetings. Rather than meeting to plan out the week's work, the animals are given orders. They also have to worship the decayed skull of Old Major, which vividly symbolizes the folly of the animals under Napoleon's rule. It expresses their ignorance in the most graphic way possible: the reverence of a hollow idealism. Major's head represents Animalism, the product of his mind. The skull represents the frame of Animalism and his brains the theory behind it, since the skull supports the head and the brains form the basis of thought. The frame of Animalism is the revolution, new social structure and everything else required to support the theory, for the theory alone cannot guide a society.

The deceased head the animals worshipped contains a skull frame, but the brains and flesh have decayed. Therefore, the animals worshipped the revolution and new social structure without realizing that the theory, or spirit, of the movement have been abandoned by their new leader, Napoleon. They celebrate their situation without realizing that the social goals they fought for are gradually disappearing under their new ruler. Their ideal is in fact dead as the head of its originator.

A close analysis of the passage supports this interpretation. The phrase "clean of flesh" serves as a euphemism for the gross state of the skull. This elegant phrasing hides the disgust of the object from the reader, as the propaganda issued by Squealer the pig hides the disgust of Napoleon's abuse of the Animalistic system from the animals. Furthermore, the skull has moved from the orchard to a tree stump. Like the skull, the state of the Animalistic society moves from a productive, growing position to a dead spot, thanks to the corrupt Napoleon. Finally, the skull now resides by and associates with the flagpole, a vehicle for propaganda and another symbol that is emptied, or "hollowed out" to show the downfall of Animal Farm.

Snowball introduces the green flag hoisted up the flagpole to celebrate Animal Farm's success each week. Its color "represent[s] the green fields of England, while [its] hoof and horn signif[y] the future Republic of Animals." (24) Its original meaning is lost when Napoleon removes the hoof and horn as one of his final acts in the work. As the now-humane swine strips the flag of its animalian features, it too becomes a hollow representation of its ideal: while meaning to symbolize the future dominance of animals, it instead ends up symbolizing their oppression. By this point, the pigs have abandoned their front legs as they have abandoned their old lifestyle, betraying the original farm commandment "whatever goes upon two legs is an enemy" (19). By removing the hoof, the animal leg marker, from the flag, the pigs remove their animal legs from the ground, leaving the rest of the farm with a dominating symbol of their betrayal. An image of an English field waves above the farm, rather than an image of the animals conquering an English field. The animals do not realize that the flag becomes devoid of proper meaning, just as they did not realize that the Animalistic façade as established by Napoleon was devoid of proper meaning. They continue to practice the tradition of hoisting the flag, again celebrating a symbol of their own demise.

After explaining his utopian dream to the animals, Old Major sings the rallying tune "Beasts of England" to them, stirring up their emotions with the almost magic anthem about the inevitable freedom they shall enjoy:

> Rings shall vanish from our noses,
>
> And the harness from our back,
>
> Bit and spur shall rust forever,
>
> Cruel whips no more shall crack.

-(Animal Farm, 9)

The song tells of a future where the objects that enslave them, such as the bit and spur, will not touch them. This song becomes the anthem of the farm and opens Sunday meetings. The animals are "taken aback" (72) when Napoleon outlaws it on account of it losing relevance to their society. He claims that it should be abolished since it strives for an ideal that has already been reached. Its replacement, "Animal Farm, Animal Farm / Never through me shalt thou come to harm" (73), gives a message with biting irony that is lost on the animals rather than an optimistic one. The animals are led to sing that Animal Farm shall never harm them, but the phrasing suggests a hidden second meaning. The pigs claim that the animals shall never harm them "through" Animal Farm; in other words, the Animal Farm's pleasant appearance prevents the subjects from protesting, so the farm itself shields the rulers. Again, the animals engage in a procedure, singing at the start of each Sunday meeting, which loses its original meaning to the hands of Napoleon's reign, while retaining some semblance of its original form similar enough not to give the plot away.

The irony of the animals worshipping the symbols of their own demise runs throughout Animal Farm, making a poignant jab on this society based around a false idealism. While the "bit and spurs" may rust forever, the political chains administered by the pigs grip the animals more tightly, as they are led to celebrate their own tragedy.

Works Cited:

Orwell, George. Animal Farm. New York: Penguin Group, 1996.

Quiz 1

1. **In Animal Farm, Orwell criticizes primarily which world leader?**
   A. Joseph Stalin
   B. Vladimir Lenin
   C. Adolf Hitler
   D. Leon Trotsky

2. **Orwell completed Animal Farm during what international conflict?**
   A. The Russo-Japanese War
   B. World War II
   C. The Cold War
   D. The Great War

3. **Animal Farm is best described as a cautionary tale against**
   A. Marxism
   B. communism
   C. totalitarianism
   D. National socialism

4. **Animal Farm fits all of the following genres except**
   A. satire
   B. allegory
   C. fable
   D. farce

5. **In what armed conflict did Orwell participate voluntarily?**
   A. the Red Terror
   B. the Spanish Civil War
   C. the February Revolution
   D. the French Congo Uprising

6. **Orwell played all of the following roles during World War II except**
   A. secret police agent
   B. propagandist
   C. member of the Home Guard
   D. war correspondent

7. **Which of the following is true of Orwell?**
   A. he was a poor student
   B. he never married
   C. he died before the age of 50
   D. he embraced luxury

8. **Before Animal Farm, Orwell was known primarily as a(n)**
   A. teacher
   B. soldier
   C. essayist
   D. member of the bourgeoisie

9. **Orwell's other extremely successul novel is called**
   A. Nineteen Eighty-Four
   B. Brave New World
   C. The Master and Margarita
   D. Harrison Bergeron

10. **In what year did the Russian Revolution occur?**
   A. 1905
   B. 1917
   C. 1924
   D. 1939

11. **The initial Soviet campaign to quash internal dissidence was called**
   A. the Red Terror
   B. the Decembrists' Revolt
   C. the Five Year Plan
   D. the Cold War

12. **What event allowed Stalin to assume Soviet leadership?**
   A. The February Revolution
   B. Hitler's ascension
   C. Lenin's death
   D. The Treaty of Brest-Litovsk

13. **What character in Animal Farm represents Karl Marx?**
   A. Old Major
   B. Benjamin
   C. Napoleon
   D. Snowball

14. **What character in Animal Farm represents Trotsky?**
   A. Napoleon
   B. Snowball
   C. Squealer
   D. Boxer

15. **What character in Animal Farm represents Stalin?**
   A. the Horse-Slaughterer
   B. Napoleon
   C. Squealer
   D. Frederick

16. **The dogs in Animal Farm can be said to represent**
   A. secret police
   B. peasants
   C. educated elites
   D. foreign diplomats

17. **What character adopts the personal maxim, "I will work harder"?**
   A. Clover
   B. Benjamin
   C. Snowball
   D. Boxer

18. **Which class of creatures stages its own small-scale rebellion against the pigs?**
   A. the hens
   B. the cows
   C. the sheep
   D. the wild rats and rabbits

19. **Squealer's job is to distribute what among the animals?**
   A. weekly assignments
   B. rations
   C. propaganda
   D. reading materials

20. **Which of the following is not a slogan in Animal Farm?**
   A. "Four legs good, two legs better"
   B. "All animals are equal / But some animals are more equal than others"
   C. "War is peace / Freedom is Slavery / Ignorance is Strength"
   D. "Long live Comrade Napoleon"

21. **Which of the following is/are most clearly an example of propaganda?**
   A. the pigs' decision to wear clothing
   B. Squealer's optimistic statistics
   C. the original Seven Commandments
   D. the reductions of rations

22. **The threat of what scares the animals into submission?**
   A. Jones's return
   B. Old Major's exhumation
   C. Pilkington's atrocities
   D. a trip to the glue factory

23. **Which of the following is NOT one of the Seven Commandments?**
   A. "No animal shall sleep in a bed"
   B. "No animal shall dishonor his father"
   C. "No animal shall drink alcohol"
   D. "No animal shall kill any other animal"

24. **The pigs break all of the Seven Commandments EXCEPT**
   A. "All animals are equal"
   B. they break all of them
   C. "No animal shall drink alcohol"
   D. "Whatever goes upon two legs is an enemy"

25. **When the animals tour the farmhouse, they discover that the Joneses lived in**
   A. denial
   B. luxury
   C. squalor
   D. sin

Quiz 1 Answer Key

1. **(A)** Joseph Stalin
2. **(B)** World War II
3. **(C)** totalitarianism
4. **(D)** farce
5. **(B)** the Spanish Civil War
6. **(A)** secret police agent
7. **(C)** he died before the age of 50
8. **(C)** essayist
9. **(A)** Nineteen Eighty-Four
10. **(B)** 1917
11. **(A)** the Red Terror
12. **(C)** Lenin's death
13. **(A)** Old Major
14. **(B)** Snowball
15. **(B)** Napoleon
16. **(A)** secret police
17. **(D)** Boxer
18. **(A)** the hens
19. **(C)** propaganda
20. **(C)** "War is peace / Freedom is Slavery / Ignorance is Strength"
21. **(B)** Squealer's optimistic statistics
22. **(A)** Jones's return
23. **(B)** "No animal shall dishonor his father"
24. **(B)** they break all of them
25. **(B)** luxury

Quiz 2

1. **Which animal is absent from Old Major's big meeting?**
   A. Mollie
   B. Clover
   C. Benjamin
   D. Moses

2. **According to old Major, what is Man?**
   A. "the thought police of animal lives"
   B. "the most mysterious animal on Earth"
   C. "the only animal that consumes without producing"
   D. "the guiding light in the quest for animal equality"

3. **Where did Old Major hear the song, "Beasts of England"?**
   A. in his home country of Russia
   B. in a dream
   C. at a state fair where he was exhibited
   D. eavesdropping outside the Joneses' kitchen

4. **According to old Major, what must the animals NOT do?**
   A. emulate human beings
   B. put their cause before themselves
   C. prepare themselves for revolution
   D. become rich and free

5. **Which of the following is true of "Beasts of England"?**
   A. it has the same tune as "Mary Had a Little Lamb"
   B. it advocates a coup d'etat against Napoleon
   C. its tune is simple enough for even the dullest animals to learn
   D. it espouses the use of deceit and terror

6. **What event gives the animals the opportunity to rebel?**
   A. Frederick attempts to seize control of Foxwood
   B. Old Major dies unexpectedly
   C. Mr. Jones neglects to feed the animals
   D. Mrs. Jones and Mr. Jones have an explosive fight

7. **In the days following the Rebellion, the animals gain a newfound sense of**
    A. terror
    B. comfort
    C. exhaustion
    D. dishonesty

8. **Who takes the cows' milk secretly after the Seven Commandments are read?**
    A. the pigs
    B. the cows
    C. the raven
    D. the farmers

9. **Which of the following is NOT proof of Animalism's effectiveness?**
    A. each animal does the task to which it is best suited
    B. the pigs add milk and apples to their rations
    C. the animals are satisfied with their rations
    D. the animals do not steal or argue

10. **Why does Snowball reduce the Seven Commandments to a single maxim?**
    A. in order to conserve the farm's paint supply, which they have no means of replenishing
    B. most of the animals are too dull to memorize more than that
    C. the sheep demand a catchier slogan that they can chant at meetings
    D. he and the other pigs decide that the Seven Commandments are flawed

11. **What symbols does the Animal Farm flag feature?**
    A. a hoof and horn
    B. a pig and sword
    C. a scythe and windmill
    D. a sword and horseshoe

12. **What character secludes the newborn puppies in a loft?**
    A. Clover
    B. Napoleon
    C. Snowball
    D. Squealer

13. **All of the following are outside reactions to Animal Farm's success EXCEPT**
    A. animals on other farms begin disobeying their owners
    B. the humans spread rumors about Animal Farm
    C. humans cut off all trade agreements with Animal Farm
    D. farmers who dislike each other unite in their hatred of Animal Farm

14. **What animal leads the charge at the Battle of the Cowshed?**
    A. Napoleon
    B. Snowball
    C. Boxer
    D. Moses

15. **What animal receives the distinction of "Animal Hero" aside from Snowball and the slain sheep?**
    A. Benjamin
    B. Napoleon
    C. Squealer
    D. Boxer

16. **What happens to Mollie?**
    A. she runs away to live a domesticated life
    B. she dies in the Battle of the Cowshed
    C. she perishes from coccidiosis
    D. she is taken away by a horse-slaughterer

17. **Over what issue do Snowball and Napoleon clash most fiercely?**
    A. elitism
    B. rations
    C. trade with humans
    D. the windmill

18. **The only animal that refuses to support either Snowball or Napoleon is**
    A. Pincher
    B. Benjamin
    C. Squealer
    D. Boxer

19. **What is Napoleon's first action after he seizes control?**
   A. he abolishes Sunday meetings
   B. he reduces rations by one third
   C. he sends the dogs to Foxwood to assassinate Snowball
   D. he changes two of the Seven Commandments

20. **What does Napoleon claim, regarding the windmill?**
   A. that it was his idea all along
   B. that building it will be impossible
   C. that it will be most useful for grinding corn
   D. that it will have magical powers

21. **What is involuntary about Napoleon's 'strictly voluntary' labor on Sundays?**
   A. there is a punishment for declining to work
   B. it is much harder labor than the animals can tolerate
   C. it is to be done without any animal standing on its hind legs
   D. it is meant to advance the goal of planting barley for whisky

22. **What do the animals use to break limestone into pieces?**
   A. the force of gravity
   B. the electricity provided by the windmill
   C. a grain elevator
   D. human tools that they find in the harness-room

23. **What about trading with humans makes the animals uneasy?**
   A. they do not understand what trading means
   B. only the pigs will benefit from trade agreements
   C. they would rather deal in cash than in goods
   D. the Seven Commandments forbid it

24. **How do the farmers react to Animal Farm's continued success?**
   A. they try to alienate Animal Farm from the outside world
   B. they are indifferent
   C. they begin to admire it
   D. they begin stockpiling weapons for an attack

25. **What news inspires Clover to review the Seven Commandments for the first time?**
   A. the pigs are sleeping in beds
   B. the pigs are learning trades
   C. the pigs are drinking alcohol
   D. the pigs are adding milk and apples to their rations

Quiz 2 Answer Key

1. **(D)** Moses
2. **(C)** "the only animal that consumes without producing"
3. **(B)** in a dream
4. **(A)** emulate human beings
5. **(C)** its tune is simple enough for even the dullest animals to learn
6. **(C)** Mr. Jones neglects to feed the animals
7. **(B)** comfort
8. **(A)** the pigs
9. **(B)** the pigs add milk and apples to their rations
10. **(B)** most of the animals are too dull to memorize more than that
11. **(A)** a hoof and horn
12. **(B)** Napoleon
13. **(C)** humans cut off all trade agreements with Animal Farm
14. **(B)** Snowball
15. **(D)** Boxer
16. **(A)** she runs away to live a domesticated life
17. **(D)** the windmill
18. **(B)** Benjamin
19. **(A)** he abolishes Sunday meetings
20. **(A)** that it was his idea all along
21. **(A)** there is a punishment for declining to work
22. **(A)** the force of gravity
23. **(D)** the Seven Commandments forbid it
24. **(C)** they begin to admire it
25. **(A)** the pigs are sleeping in beds

Quiz 3

1. **Whom does Napoleon blame for the windmill's destruction?**
   A. the rebellious hens
   B. Snowball
   C. the four dissenting pigs
   D. Boxer

2. **What does Napoleon do to falsely convince the outside world of Animal Farm's prosperity?**
   A. he executes animals in order to decrease the farm's population
   B. he shows Whymper the food bins, which are made to look full
   C. he sends Squealer to town to read false statistics to the humans
   D. he reduces rations in order to send more goods to Willingdon

3. **Napoleon forces the hens to sell their eggs in order to pay for**
   A. sheets
   B. medicine
   C. machinery
   D. grain

4. **What is one of the hens' tactics of defiance during their strike?**
   A. they lay their eggs in the rafters
   B. they hatch their eggs at record speed
   C. they spread coccidiosis to the other animals
   D. they throw eggs at the farmhouse

5. **How does Napoleon retaliate against the hens?**
   A. he murders every one of them
   B. he buys new hens
   C. he stops their rations
   D. he adds eggs to the pigs' rations

6. **Napoleon negotiates with Frederick and Pilkington, who want to buy Animal Farm's supply of**
   A. barley
   B. timber
   C. cow's milk
   D. limestone

7. **Napoleon conducts a public inspection of whose secret activities?**
   A. Jones's
   B. Snowball's
   C. Frederick's
   D. Pilkington's

8. **Boxer protests the idea that**
   A. Snowball was on Jones's side in the Battle of the Cowshed
   B. the pigs should be allowed to drink alcohol
   C. the windmill was never Snowball's idea
   D. Napoleon is always right

9. **At the assembly, why don't the dogs drag Boxer out to confess?**
   A. he has already been taken away
   B. he is too strong for them
   C. he is lying in his stall, injured
   D. he has said nothing wrong

10. **On whom do the 'traitorous' animals blame their misdeeds?**
   A. Napoleon
   B. Snowball
   C. Frederick
   D. Jones

11. **Despite the terror of the public executions, Clover believes that**
   A. the animals are better off than they were in Jones's days
   B. the animals are not to blame for the evil influences among them
   C. the pigs are misleading the animals deliberately
   D. Snowball should have been the leader of Animal Farm

12. **According to Squealer, what did the executions end?**
   A. the Rebellion
   B. the period of hardship
   C. the Battle of the Cowshed
   D. the Battle of the Windmill

13. **According to Squealer, why are the animals not to sing "Beasts of England" anymore?**
    A. it is obsolete
    B. it is an ugly song
    C. it is pessimistic
    D. it resembles human songs

14. **What character has composed Animal Farm's new anthem?**
    A. Pinkeye
    B. Minimus
    C. Napoleon
    D. Squealer

15. **What does Napoleon have inscribed on the barn wall opposite the Seven Commandments?**
    A. "God Save the Queen"
    B. "Beasts of England"
    C. "Comrade Napoleon"
    D. "Clementine"

16. **To whom does Napoleon agree to sell the timber first?**
    A. Whymper
    B. Frederick
    C. Pilkington
    D. Jones

17. **What does Frederick purportedly do to his animals?**
    A. torture them
    B. slaughter them using new, 'humane' methods
    C. allow them to run their own affairs
    D. sell them in exchange for whisky

18. **To whom does Napoleon end up selling the timber?**
    A. Whymper
    B. Frederick
    C. Pilkington
    D. Jones

19. **What does Napoleon refuse to accept as payment for the timber?**
   A. a check
   B. a newborn foal
   C. a case of whisky
   D. a supply of grain

20. **What does Napoleon promise to buy with the payment for the timber?**
   A. machinery for the windmill
   B. weapons for the farm's defense
   C. a grain elevator
   D. a threshing machine

21. **Why can't the pigs use the banknotes?**
   A. animals are not allowed to deal with money
   B. the banknotes are forgeries
   C. the banknotes disappear mysteriously
   D. the pigs cannot go to Willingdon by themselves

22. **Pilkington sends a note to Napoleon that says**
   A. "We declare war"
   B. "All animals are equal"
   C. "Serves you right"
   D. "Long live Comrade Snowball"

23. **Who leads the second attack on Animal Farm?**
   A. Snowball
   B. Frederick
   C. Pilkington
   D. Jones

24. **What animal is conspicously missing from the Battle of the Windmill?**
   A. Muriel
   B. Napoleon
   C. Squealer
   D. Boxer

25. **What does the enemy do to the windmill?**

A. steals it
B. weakens it
C. blows it up
D. graffitis it

Quiz 3 Answer Key

1. **(B)** Snowball
2. **(B)** he shows Whymper the food bins, which are made to look full
3. **(D)** grain
4. **(A)** they lay their eggs in the rafters
5. **(C)** he stops their rations
6. **(B)** timber
7. **(B)** Snowball's
8. **(A)** Snowball was on Jones's side in the Battle of the Cowshed
9. **(B)** he is too strong for them
10. **(B)** Snowball
11. **(A)** the animals are better off than they were in Jones's days
12. **(A)** the Rebellion
13. **(A)** it is obsolete
14. **(B)** Minimus
15. **(C)** "Comrade Napoleon"
16. **(C)** Pilkington
17. **(A)** torture them
18. **(B)** Frederick
19. **(A)** a check
20. **(A)** machinery for the windmill
21. **(B)** the banknotes are forgeries
22. **(C)** "Serves you right"
23. **(B)** Frederick
24. **(C)** Squealer
25. **(C)** blows it up

Quiz 4

1. **Whom does Napoleon award the honor "Order of the Green Banner"?**
   A. himself
   B. a sheep, posthumously
   C. Squealer
   D. Boxer

2. **What does Napoleon mistake for the onset of death?**
   A. hallucinations
   B. coccidiosis
   C. hypothermia
   D. drunkenness

3. **After he recovers, Napoleon begins researching**
   A. how to stand on two legs
   B. how to brew liquor
   C. how to stamp out the enemy
   D. how to build a stronger windmill

4. **When referring to rations, what word does Squealer use in place of "reduced"?**
   A. "reciprocated"
   B. "reupholstered"
   C. "retaliated"
   D. "readjusted"

5. **How does Napoleon obtain thirty-one young pigs for the farm?**
   A. he recruits them from other farms
   B. he purchases them from Pilkington
   C. he parents them
   D. he steals them from Frederick

6. **What does Napoleon plan to build for the young pigs?**
   A. a schoolhouse
   B. a liquor distillation system
   C. a windmill
   D. a tailor shop

7. **Aside from the pigs, which is the only animal allowed a ration of beer?**
   A. Benjamin
   B. Bluebell
   C. Boxer
   D. Moses

8. **Which of the following is true?**
   A. the pigs learn the trade of veterinary medicine
   B. when times are hard, the pigs reduce their own privileges
   C. the hens are able to regroup despite the egg quotas
   D. the animals enjoy the Spontaneous Demonstrations

9. **Napoleon awards the pigs all of the following privileges EXCEPT**
   A. consuming sugar
   B. wearing ribbons in their tails
   C. eating meat
   D. the right of way on the path

10. **Boxer collapses from**
   A. the injury to his hoof
   B. overwork
   C. disillusionment
   D. drunkenness

11. **What does Boxer vow to do in his final days?**
   A. finish building the schoolhouse
   B. confess to treachery
   C. take revenge on Napoleon
   D. learn the alphabet

12. **Which character reads the lettering on the side of the horse-slaughterer's van?**
   A. Clover
   B. Muriel
   C. Benjamin
   D. Moses

13. **Why does Boxer fail to escape from the van?**
    A. he has grown too weak
    B. he does not know to try
    C. the van is made of steel
    D. the van is surrounded by armed guards

14. **Two horses draw the horse-slaughterer's van. This is an example of**
    A. simile
    B. metonymy
    C. personification
    D. irony

15. **Accoring to Squealer, Boxer died**
    A. defiant of Animalism
    B. despite receiving the best possible care
    C. before he reached Willingdon
    D. for profit and the public good

16. **According to Squealer, Boxer's last words**
    A. marked him as a traitor
    B. expressed his love for Clover
    C. glorified the cause of Animalism
    D. referred to Sugarcandy Mountain

17. **On the day appointed for Boxer's memorial banquet, what arrives from town?**
    A. a giant wreath
    B. a crate of horseshoes
    C. a case of whisky
    D. a shipment of glue

18. **Which of the following animals dies by the end of the book?**
    A. Clover
    B. Muriel
    C. Benjamin
    D. Moses

19. **By the end of the book, Animal Farm features all of the following EXCEPT**
    A. additional land
    B. a grain elevator
    C. a windmill
    D. electricity

20. **According to Napoleon, the truest happiness lies in**
    A. working hard and living frugally
    B. glorifying his name forever
    C. defeating enemies to the cause of Animalism
    D. ascending Sugarcandy Mountain

21. **All of the following keep the animals from feeling the full brunt of their hardship EXCEPT**
    A. ignorance
    B. education
    C. propaganda
    D. pride

22. **What chant does Squealer teach the sheep?**
    A. "Four legs good, two legs better!"
    B. "Some animals are more equal than others!"
    C. "Long live Comrade Napoleon!""
    D. "Animal Farm, never shalt thou come to harm!"

23. **Who reads Animal Farm's new, single maxim to Clover?**
    A. she reads it herself
    B. Muriel
    C. Benjamin
    D. Moses

24. **When the animals peer into the farmhouse, what do they see the pigs and humans doing together?**
    A. dining
    B. writing a manifesto
    C. warring
    D. copulating

25. **Pilkington announces his plan to**

A. take control of Pinchfield
B. emulate Napoleon's policies
C. buy a stake in Animal Farm
D. publicly humiliate Jones

Quiz 4 Answer Key

1. **(A)** himself
2. **(D)** drunkenness
3. **(B)** how to brew liquor
4. **(D)** "readjusted"
5. **(C)** he parents them
6. **(A)** a schoolhouse
7. **(D)** Moses
8. **(D)** the animals enjoy the Spontaneous Demonstrations
9. **(C)** eating meat
10. **(B)** overwork
11. **(D)** learn the alphabet
12. **(C)** Benjamin
13. **(A)** he has grown too weak
14. **(D)** irony
15. **(B)** despite receiving the best possible care
16. **(C)** glorified the cause of Animalism
17. **(C)** a case of whisky
18. **(B)** Muriel
19. **(D)** electricity
20. **(A)** working hard and living frugally
21. **(B)** education
22. **(A)** "Four legs good, two legs better!"
23. **(C)** Benjamin
24. **(A)** dining
25. **(B)** emulate Napoleon's policies

Quiz 5

1. **By the end of the book, Napoleon has done all of the following EXCEPT**
   A. change the farm's flag
   B. acquire the title-deeds to the farm
   C. restore the farm's original name
   D. admit to his tactics of deception

2. **At the book's end, the pigs are**
   A. a force that cannot possibly be overthrown
   B. transformed into human beings
   C. indistinguishable from humans
   D. wealthier than the humans

Quiz 5 Answer Key

1. **(D)** admit to his tactics of deception
2. **(C)** indistinguishable from humans

ClassicNotes

GradeSaver™

Getting you the grade since 1999™

Other ClassicNotes from GradeSaver™

Things Fall Apart
The Threepenny Opera
Thus Spoke Zarathustra
The Time Machine
Titus Andronicus
To Build a Fire
To Kill a Mockingbird
To the Lighthouse
Treasure Island
Troilus and Cressida
Turn of the Screw
Twelfth Night
Ulysses
Uncle Tom's Cabin
Utopia
A Very Old Man With Enormous Wings
Villette
The Visit
Volpone
Waiting for Godot
Waiting for Lefty
Walden
Washington Square
The Waste Land
Where the Red Fern Grows
White Fang
White Noise
White Teeth
Who's Afraid of Virginia Woolf
Wide Sargasso Sea
Winesburg, Ohio
The Winter's Tale
The Woman Warrior
Wordsworth's Poetical Works
Woyzeck
Wuthering Heights
The Yellow Wallpaper
Yonnondio: From the Thirties

52946572R00066

Made in the USA
Middletown, DE
23 November 2017